To Bob & Georgie

As an appreciation of a lovely holiday spent at their beautiful home:—

"SCOTCHELLS"

from MABEL.

<small>GENERAL EDITOR</small>: John Sales, Garden Adviser, National Trust

Dorset, Hampshire and the Isle of Wight

Allen Paterson

In association with the Royal Horticultural Society

B.T. Batsford Ltd, *London*

For Penelope
who encouraged and typed

First published 1978

© Allen Paterson 1978

ISBN 0 7134 0992 4

Filmset by Servis Filmsetting Ltd, Manchester
Printed in Great Britain by
J.W. Arrowsmith Ltd, Bristol
for the publisher,
B.T. Batsford Ltd,
4 Fitzhardinge St, LondonW1H 0AH

Contents

List of Illustrations

List of Garden Plans

Acknowledgments

The Author and Publisher would like to thank Patrick Leeson for all plans and Tania Midgley for colour plates 1, 2 and 4.

Preface

Garden visiting has almost become a national sport in recent years. It is associated of course with the availability to the public of stately homes in private ownership or in the care of the National Trust, and others. But enjoyable and instructive though this is, it is seldom one can feel personally involved with what one sees; the Great Saloon at X has remarkably little connection with the sittingroom at home, nor is the famous 'Parterre de Broderie' on the Garden Front at Y immediately redolent of our own patch.

This is why the current access to numbers of gardens, possibly only for one day in the year is so exciting. There is always something to which we can relate, which we can adapt for ourselves. And occasionally there is the feeling (not infrequently loudly voiced by visitors, as those who open their gardens know) that one's own herbaceous border is *just* as good 'and just look at the plantains in this lawn!'.

The majority of gardens described in this book are relatively small and hence personal. Visitors should, while not leaving critical faculties at the gate, try to accept the raison d'être for each garden and look at it with understanding eyes. This helps one to see one's own, on returning home, with a clearer vision – though sometimes, it must be said, with a strong feeling of depression.

Our thanks, then, with the 20p or whatever in the collecting box, must go to the owners. Also to the National Gardens Scheme organised by and for the Queen's Institute of District Nursing which instituted the scheme in 1927. Now over 1200 gardens open each year on its behalf. Its annual 'Yellow Book' is a vital part of the travelling gardener's equipment. Other charities, such as The Gardeners' Benevolent Society and the Order of St John also have schemes which give information of what is open when.

In the pages which follow, detailed descriptions are given of gardens of Southern England which were open in 1975 and 1976. Gardening is the most transient art; plants die, owners sell up and move so no guarantee is given that all of these gardens will continue to be available. The annual schedules of the charities *must* be consulted.

It should also be emphasised that the descriptions give a personal view – while attempting a balanced one – and personal enthusiasms and prejudices are bound to show through.

It remains to record sincere thanks to all those garden owners and gardeners in Southern England for their kindness and welcoming hospitality during the time this book was being prepared and to hope that they, and others, will continue to provide this feast for visitors year after year.

Allen Paterson

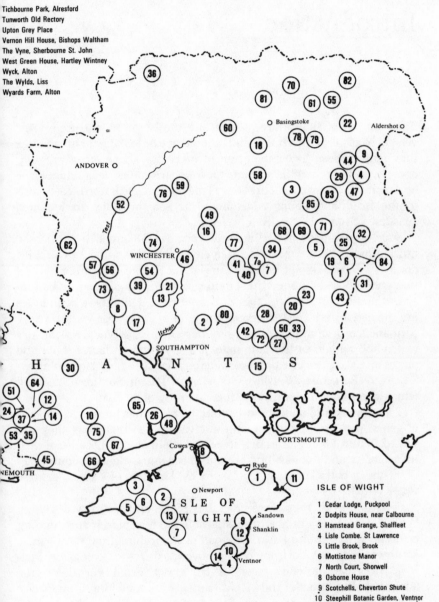

Introduction

The counties of Hampshire, Dorset and the Isle of Wight occupy the central block of southern England. Should one be looking for an analogy they may be seen in combination to make the shape of an irregular boot; Lyme Regis is at the extreme toe to the west, the Isle of Wight is the heel to the east from which the back of the boot proceeds north-eastwards to the heathland above Aldershot. The sole provides an indented coastline of some 150 miles in extent.

Such a metaphor is perhaps not very elegant but if it provides a quick mind's eye picture of the area covered by this survey it will have done its job; we are apt in these times of local government reorganisation and imposed bureaucratic change to forget the old county boundaries and the individualities they encompass. No doubt these boundaries are themselves arbitrary bureaucratic lines of a past age yet their very permanence over hundreds of years has encouraged local specificities which still remain in the language, if less so now in fact. People and places and attitudes are, or were, different across the borders in Surrey, Sussex, or Berkshire, Wiltshire, Somerset or Devon. Southern England, which these counties surround, has an entity of its own.

Topography and geology, predating men's minds by untold millions of years, pay no attention to these divisions yet inevitably they are linked. Natural boundaries of a river or a chain of hills, because of their invariability and defensibility, are apt to become the logical boundaries of a tribe or petty kingdom. This is the old kingdom of Wessex, centred upon Winchester.

Geographically, these three counties make up a country of rolling chalk downs, rising in height to almost 1000 ft in places, surrounding the central Hampshire Basin. One half of Hampshire, from Basingstoke southwards to the Portsdown ridge overlooking the Solent and Spithead (a great drowned river) is chalkland. From Portsdown the further chalk heights of the Wight can be seen stretching from Culver Cliff in the east to (on a *very* fine day) the Needles at the western extremity; from here, across the broad expanse of Poole Bay the chalk can be picked up again at St Albans Head and can be followed along the line of the Purbeck Hills to Dorchester. The western Downs now sweep north-eastwards through Milton Abbas and Blandford Forum to Cranbourne Chase on the southern edge of Salisbury Plain. This in turn, cut by the classic chalk streams of the Hampshire Avon and the Test, joins the main body of the Hampshire Downs. Chalk both makes and encloses these counties.

It provides a very typical landscape of open arable lands – though the great sheep runs are no more – hangers of beech and a most delightful natural flora; orchids, harebells, scabious and corn-flowers, whitebeam and juniper. It is still largely unspoiled, although with the vast population increase of the last two decades the pressures upon it are enormous (population of Hampshire, Dorset and the Isle of Wight approaches 2,000,000).

Mr Ralph Dutton in his *Hinton Ampner, a Hampshire Manor* (Batsford 1968) suggests, in describing the rural charms of his deeply loved bit of chalkland Hampshire, that he 'resembles William Curtis, a famous son of Hampshire, who in the years following 1777 detailed in his *Flora Londinensis* the many wild flowers he found in the fields of Battersea and Bermondsey which were soon to disappear beneath bricks and mortar'. Heaven preserve these counties from a similar fate.

Paul Nash, who wrote and illustrated the excellent first Shell Guide to Dorset in 1935 was already then concerned about the dangers of despoliation of Dorset and its still Hardyesque way of life; he dedicated his book to 'all those courageous enemies of development'.

On the mainland coastal strip this battle, if it can be so called, is clearly lost. Portsmouth and Southampton are virtually one and a vast suburban sprawl spreads from Christchurch through Bournemouth to Poole and inland to Ringwood. We should bless the West Saxon kings and later William the Conqueror in 1079 for causing the great tract of land between these two twentieth-century conurbations to be placed under the forest laws. What was then named the New Forest is now an invaluable lung for the whole area.

With the emphasis upon chalklands a possibly monotonous similarity could be expected in natural flora and the necessarily lime-tolerant plants of chalkland gardens. But dominance does not spell exclusivity, as the visitor to the New Forest knows. Here are 130 square miles of acid sandy heath, much planted by the Forestry Commission which administers three-quarters of the area. It provides sites for some of the greatest collections of rhododendrons and other calcifuge plants in the country.

Further west, inside the Dorchester–Cranbourne–Studland triangle is Thomas Hardy's Egdon Heath, sometimes called the 'New Forest of

Dorset' with similarly poor agricultural potential but offering interesting opportunities to gardeners and to garden visitors.

Where the chalk dips it is often overlaid with later Tertiary soils, both sands and clays. This is particularly apparent in the Isle of Wight which possesses in fact a unique geological structure having many different rocks in its small area (it is only 22 miles east-west and 13 miles north-south). The multi-coloured sandstone cliffs of Alum Bay are especially well known. Although the chalk still dominates – St Boniface Down reaches 787 ft in height – faults and erosions offer a surprising diversity. The north side with its heavier soils is more naturally treed while on the south, pounded by the seas of the English Channel (and Cherbourg is just 60 miles due south) is the extraordinary Undercliff. Here are a series of terraces, formed by the slipping of both chalk and Upper Greensand over Gault Clay. Streams have cut the famous chines at Shanklin and Black Gang.

The Undercliff faces due south, is protected by the high downs behind and enjoys a microclimate which is a gardener's dream. The potential for succeeding with the tender exotic trees and shrubs that used to be the prerogative of Tresco in the Scillies is beginning to be exploited by Ventnor Botanic Garden.

The oldest rocks in the three counties are on the eastern boundary of Hampshire which can be seen as the western end of the Weald of Kent and Sussex. Here are the often horticulturally covetable Lower and Upper Greensands which happily permit plants from both ends of the pH spectrum.

North east of the main chalk massif an odd corner of Hampshire seems not quite to belong. The rivers, the Wey, the Loddon and the Blackwater untypically flow northwards into the Thames Basin. Where there is greensand as at Bentley and Binsted fine gardens are made but where the thin, highly acid Bagshot Sands take over difficulties are compounded by the surprisingly severe climate.

Climatically, the southern England of these counties is predictable. January isotherms in Britain follow a generally northwest-southeast direction becoming colder from west to east. The 39°F line thus cuts off this north east corner of Hampshire whilst west Dorset is inside the 42°F belt. Rainfall is within the 28–34 inch range, a narrow coastal strip from Portland eastwards being at the lower end. But gardens and what they can grow are a product, not just of generalised trends but of the fascinating local combinations of aspect, soil, exposure, and shelter which tend to modify or exaggerate the bigger facts. Hence every garden is an individual (even the two gardens of a pair of semi-detached villas sharing a dividing fence face different ways) and the product of individual taste and inclination. In the descriptions of the gardens which follow no apology is made for emphasising the unusual or reputably tender shrubs that are seen time and again. Such plants no doubt show this to be a relatively favoured area of the country; but knowledge of their presence may encourage also the more frequent planting of such things not just in other gardens of southern England but in further areas as well.

With very few exceptions these gardens are not of great historical connection. One might see the removal of the capital of England and of the court from Winchester to London in the twelfth century as the end of more than two millenia of social significance. Vestiges of the importance early peoples assigned to the area remain with the hill-forts distributed on eminences throughout the chalklands. They culminate perhaps in the great earthworks of Maiden Castle near Dorchester whose outer circle, enclosing 130 acres, is two miles in extent. Here were a series of occupations from 2000 B.C. to Roman times and beyond.

The Romans themselves left at Portchester the sea-washed flint walls and bastions which are the best-preserved fortifications of their period in this country. (Not surprisingly, no useful vestiges of Roman horticultural enterprises remain to us as, for example, at Pompeii; but just across the county boundary at Fishbourne near Chichester is a recent recreation of a Roman colonial garden at the excavated Palace.)

Even nearer our own time this is not an area of great palatial houses surrounded by the ghosts of vanished parterres. However, Dorset, in particular, is packed with lovely manor houses which invariably combine vernacular architecture with local materials in a completely satisfying way. Their gardens are frequently in keeping. Yet for the students of early garden history these counties are a disappointment. Gardens of the monastic houses which moved into private hands at the Dissolution are products of a later age, eighteenth century at Mottisfont and mainly later still at Beaulieu and Forde.

The eighteenth century is better represented with fine Capability Brown landscapes at Broadlands and Highclere (at Warnford the house is demolished but a visit to the parish church in the Park, especially lovely at snowdrop time, shows the remains of another. It is, of course, when his work becomes virtually indistinguishable from that of 'Nature' that Brown's genius is most clearly felt). There are remnants of seven other Brown landscapes in Hampshire (Miss Dorothy Stroud's book should be consulted for details), and he also worked on Appuldur-combe in the Isle of Wight. Only two sites in Dorset claimed his attention: Milton Abbey and Sherbourne – both are superb examples. Surprisingly, Humphrey Repton who took up Brown's mantle, is virtually unrepresented. He was consulted over Stratton Park in Hampshire but the job was not executed. In the Isle of Wight he designed for St John's and may have assisted with the grounds at Nash's own East Cowes Castle.

With the rise of fashionable sea-bathing came the development of several late eighteenth-century and early nineteenth-century watering-places which still hold their delicate charm. Weymouth has become rather big but Lyme Regis, as redolent of Miss Austen as Chawton itself, offers much to the garden visitor. No open garden appears in the lists but the association of plants, however fortuitously, with quietly good architecture appears on all sides. The mildness of the spot is emphasised by the quivering shadows of eucalyptus falling upon Regency stucco or the sharpness of phormium leaves against a swelling bay window.

It is the nineteenth century and the first decades of our own which provide gardens in southern England to rival any in the country. New species from new lands beyond the seas flooded into Britain and areas of the country with climates known to be climatically favoured provided them with suitable homes. Abbotsbury, that great houseless garden inside the Chesil Bank gave a lead. Further north Minterne took some of the first Hooker Arboreum rhododendrons from the Himalayas, upon which was built a notable collection of this genus. Pylewell and Exbury on the Solent shore of the New Forest have been noted rhododendron gardens for over half a century.

Plantsmanship, then, has been and is a feature of the gardens of southern England. Yet this should not be and seldom is merely the efficient cultivation of esoteric rarities. It is the successful blending of species, growing them happily together in order to build satisfying garden pictures. These are developed to fulfil the especial need of an owner or requirements of a family. This is why such a diversity of styles is possible. Gertrude Jekyll, an initiator in such thought was typically dogmatic: 'I am strongly of the opinion the possession of a quantity of plants, however good the plants may be in themselves and however ample their number, does not make a garden; it only makes a collection!' There are several of Miss Jekyll's gardens at Burley in the New Forest. From the visitor's point of view size of garden is of little significance; a small garden can offer as much of interest as broad acres; only the scale is different.

Indeed, in these days of economy when maintenance, even with modern aids, is a major problem, the smaller, mainly owner-maintained garden has decided advantages. And perhaps because it is easier to cherish and cosset a plant close at hand the small garden can often show plants that would be the envy of Adam himself. I think particularly of the specimen of *Camellia reticulata* at Calluna. Chandlers Ford. Acreage then is not of necessity important, quality is; and of this invaluable commodity the Gardens of Southern England have more than their share.

The Gardens of Dorset

Abbotsbury

1 mile W of village of Abbotsbury (B3157); take the road to Chesil Beach and sea. Open mid-March to end of September, weekdays 10–5.30, Sundays 2–7. October to mid-March 10–5.

Everyone knows of the remarkable swannery at Abbotsbury; just as remarkable (and to gardeners more so) are the Abbotsbury Gardens beyond the village.

The whole ambiance is extraordinary. A narrow road drops down towards the sea, which is entirely hidden behind the Chesil Beach – that great 10 mile shingle bank curving from Portland Bill along the edge of Lyme Bay. Suddenly huge trees arch the lane and the Gardens' gates appear.

Here are no grounds around a stately home but a stately garden in its own right, some 17 acres of dense woodland which has been planted, from the seventeenth century onward, to give shelter from the salty gales and provide an enviable microclimate; virtually frost-free, high humidity – though only a 27 in rainfall, and an organic soil with a pH reading of 4–5. What more can keen gardeners want? The answer is money; maintenance costs in such a site are enormous and for years Abbotsbury just ticked over whilst huge trees fell into the lake – and the forest of camellias tangled their branches high above the heads of incredulous visitors, but now under an enthusiastic head gardener the place is moving forward again.

At the gate is one of the few level pieces of ground; to the left it rises up a steep bank, while ahead a flight of steps drops to the walled garden. Peacocks usually decorate the piers and appear again and again as one wanders around. The walled garden holds camellias, towards 100 years old and 20 ft in height. Mimosas are twice that, as is *Magnolia campbellii* which is worth making a country-long pilgrimage to see in early March. (But better enquire first whether it is out or over before embarking on one. Flowering time can vary season by season.) Here too are huge – and most of Abbotsbury's mature specimens earn that epithet – *Cornus kousa* and *C.nuttallii*. *Magnolia delavayi* is an open ground 30-footer. Note the several trachycarpus palms with hairy trunks like legs of giant orang-utans.

West of the walled garden are interesting plants amid a circle of aged cannons but the bulk of the developing planting is on the south east side. Here the paths follow a stream, dammed at intervals. Trees are often so large that it is difficult to identify them and even more difficult to believe the identification; *Cupressus macrocarpa* planted to mark the coronation of King George V, *Ailanthus altissima, Pterocarya fraxinifolia* (wing nut), *Pinus radiata* and ginkgos seed themselves about.

Near the end of the pool path a steep flight of steps ascends the bank through hydrangeas and other shrubs. The steps are virtually stepping stones, each being made of a section of tree trunk inserted upright, one above the next. On the ridge, amongst a high shelter belt of holm oaks the visitor returns first along the line of the stream then is taken away from it to sloping sheltered lawns. Here are specimens of one of the most beautiful small trees these islands can grow – the Chilean myrtle, *Myrtus apiculata* (*M.luma*). Good at all seasons, they are 20 ft high evergreens, starred with white flowers in early summer but their pride of place comes from the elegant cinnamon trunk and branches. Low winter sun lights this to the best Cuban mahogany.

In this area too are good plants of *Cornus capitata*, possibly the finest of its genus but sadly tender for general use. Here this Himalayan earns its keep twice over; in June with its sulphur yellow 'flowers' (actually a group of tiny true flowers surrounded by sulphur yellow bracts) and in October with its large strawberry-like fruits. Nearby is the best specimen of *Acacia baileyana*, the Cootamundra wattle, I have seen outside in this country. Towards 20 ft high with bright blue glaucous feathery leaves it is remarkable at any time; when these are half hidden by clear yellow 'mimosa' the effect is quite extraordinary.

But then that is what is expected at Abbotsbury and few visitors are disappointed. Many of the rare plants are being propagated and can be purchased for the adventurous to try in their own, possibly less ideal, garden sites.

NOTEWORTHY SPECIMENS: Too many to list.

Athelhampton House

½ mile E of Puddletown on Dorchester–Bournemouth road (A35). Open April–September inclusive, Wednesdays, Thursdays, and Sundays. 10 acres. Fine medieval house also shown.

The complicated architectural plan of the mainly sixteenth-century Athelhampton House is well matched by the still developing gardens, themselves as interestingly diverse in design and plant material. Most of the formal areas around the house are the work of Inigo Thomas in the 1890's. Hence, with some earlier trees of note and thick belt woodland planting, house and gardens are admirably linked.

Entrance is by the Great Gate which faces the south front of the house. To the left a screen of Gothic arches are the remains of a Victorian greenhouse. Between these and the thatched stable block a brick path leads through shrubs to a focal point of *Tilia petiolaris*. Beyond lies the river walk. A fine circular dovecote and aged mulberry lie nearby.

But the main gardens are to the right of the gate, thus in a line with or to the east of the house. An early opening leads to the raised walks of a square formal garden with a pool and fountain. A dozen huge yew pyramids, 10 ft wide at the base and twice that high stand sentinel. To the west a flight of steps rises to a broad paved terrace. Obelisks on the balustrade repeat the shape of the yews and two tall gazebos in a French Renaissance manner have high roofs which take up the pyramidal theme again. The raised walks and this top terrace cleverly provide contours to an otherwise flat site.

Views are now obtained eastwards to the Corona – a small circular pool garden whose surrounding walls, obelisk-topped, are backed with even higher yew hedges. The planting here is tight and extravagant; permanent shrubs – eucryphias, hebes, *Daphne odora*, hoherias, *Itea ilicifolia* with long green catkins in August, variegated buddleia, *Mahonia lomariifolia* are helped (if help were needed) by cannas and chlorophytum in season. This little area is worth a lot of attention.

If the exit to the right (east) is taken, another small garden appears with some interesting plants and a pair of topiary peafowl; a lion's head spouting water makes a focal point. Beyond and through an arch is a young lime walk, presided over by a cross-looking marble Queen Victoria at the south end.

Turning north towards a classical cast of Hygea placed to balance Her Imperial Majesty, one comes level with the central porch of the east front of the house. This is glimpsed through a high wall and over-hanging trees. Continuing the vista to the right is a long canal. An eye-catcher is planned for the end.

The canal has on its north side the high wall of the kitchen garden planted with magnolias. Here the two evergreens *M.grandiflora* and *M.delavayi* can be compared. A green tunnel of apples leads through the kitchen garden past a central pool with sundial with four gnomons to a modern version of an orangery, a three-quarter span aluminium house some 75 yards long. This is planted with tender shrubs.

A path through the west wall (by which *Leycesteria formosa* looks unusually lush) leads via a development of pleached lime arches to the White Garden. The huge variegated *Acer pseudoplantanus 'leopoldii'* makes a white garden tree par excellence.

From here an entrance gate gives into the broad lawns with a long pool at the east front which was seen earlier from the canal. Against the house is a loquat and an arbour, making a summer dining room of fruiting grape-vines. This area and indeed much of the house is dominated by a vast cedar in the dense shade of which grow *Cotoneaster lactea*, variegated Elaeagnus, *Ribes laurifolium* and, against the darkest wall the evergreen climbing hydrangea *Pileostegia viburnoides*. The success of these plants here is a surprise.

NOTEWORTHY SPECIMENS: Monterey pine, *Liquidambar styraciflua*.

Cerne Abbey

8 miles N of Dorchester, W of A352. Abbey in centre of village.

The garden here falls into three parts around the house which faces the visitor at the top of Church Street. Through a wall to the left lawns are surrounded by sweeping borders of shrubs and herbaceous material. Rhododendrons have been planted in prepared soil and do surprisingly well as does *Mahonia lomariifolia* and *Ozothamnus rosmanifolius*, an unusual Australasian composite. At the west end of a small pool grows a good young plant of Brewer's weeping spruce.

Back across the road a shrub walk leads round a pond with gunnera and peltiphyllum. A broad herbaceous garden slopes down to the water edged by a rock-rose-draped retaining wall.

Behind the house (note *Actinidia kolomikta* with pink-tipped leaves on the south and a group of rhododendrons and *Camellia x williamsii* on the north) are the Abbey ruins set in a mass of cherries and other trees. *Viburnum x carlecephalum* and *Clematis armandii* are on the south wall of the gatehouse. The roof of the monks' guesthouse where Margaret of Anjou stayed during the Wars of the Roses is covered completely with polypody fern.

Chedington Court

Nr Beaminster. Turn W off A356 Dorchester–Crewkerne road at Wynyards Gap, 5 miles S of Crewkerne.

The splendidly theatrical 1820's Jacobean house in golden Ham stone is perched three-quarters of the way up the scarp slope of the last out-thrust of the Dorset Uplands.

Views to the north over the plain of Somerset are dramatic, framed and emphasised as they are by great trees contemporary, no doubt, with the house. Behind it, clustering close is the pretty village, all overhung by a great beech hanger.

The 7 acres of garden is suitably big in treatment. A top terrace on the north and west sides is supported by three yard high retaining walls. Plants on the more difficult north side include roses and clematis, garrya, *Azara microphylla* and *Vitis coignetiae*. Under the west wall *Amaryllis belladonna* is a feature in September. All round are billowing heaps of clipped yew and box, especially fine around a venerable yew on a lower lawn which gives shade to numbers of seventeenth-century tombstones marking the site of the now removed mediaeval church.

Below, a spring giving into a pair of pools is the source of the River Parrott which eventually finds the sea at Burnham on Sea. By the upper pool grows *Eucryphia glutinosa* and a huge *Pinus' mugo* now dwarfing its site. Water falls from the lower pool into a well-contrived rocky ravine planted with ferns and dwarf rhododendrons and azaleas. Here are large plants of *Cornus mas* and grey-leaved *Hippophae rhamnoides*. As a specimen of this age, sea buckthorn is a worthwhile garden plant.

Bulbs in grass surround the mown areas. Views of the house from here, seen piled up above variously shaped topiary, are especially fine.

Compton Acres

Canford Cliffs Road, Poole. From the Poole–Bournemouth road turn S into
Canford Cliffs Road.

Here are 15 enviable acres of pinewood around and in a steep glen
overlooking Poole Harbour. Through the boughs are lovely views to
Brownsea Island and across the water to the distant Isle of Purbeck. The
climate is kind and the acid soil, though not naturally rich, is ideal for
calcifuge plants.

There are many fine ideas. A long central pool in the Italian Garden
has an equally architectural backdrop of clipped *Rhododendron ponticum*
and golden conifers. *Clematis montana* in spring hangs in great swags
along its length of pergola.

Beyond, an extensive rock and water garden has variable routes to
enable every visitor to walk to his own capabilities. Good specimens of
dwarf conifers and other mature plantings cause the fill-in of bright
annual material to appear incongruous. One path leads down to the
valley floor whilst others remain above and lead to fine viewing points.
A heather dell and a bank filled with interesting cacti (presumably
treated as seasonals) are passed before entering the Japanese Garden.
This, although far removed from the spareness of any original, is
visually excellent. Water, stepping stones, garden pavilions and
interesting plants combine to make it a most successful pastiche from
whichever point it is viewed.

Cranborne Manor

From A354 Salisbury–Blandford Forum Rd take B3081 S towards Ringwood.
Turn left onto B3078 signed Cranborne.

A steep gravelled drive, shaded by high beeches drops down from the
B3078 road. At the bottom a pair of little square brick lodges stand
angled to the main line. Beyond their linking arch lies the great towered
stone major house of Cranborne, originally a hunting-box of King John.

Beneath mature trees and on rough-mown banks native and introduced shade-tolerant flowers cover the ground in spring and early summer; bulbs of all kinds, cyclamen, anemones, cowslips and fritillaries provide colour from February to June.

South east of the lodges by a huge holm oak a gap opens into a beech hedge anteroom – no flower colour, just greens and an eighteenth-century hunter in stone.

The border concentrates on summer effect; Judas trees at each end, underplanted with hellebores, *Feijoa sellowiana* (a surprising Brazilian, for this is not a warm area), hoheria, *Viburnum burkwoodii* and a big summer flowering magnolia. Below are peonies, roses (both bushes and climbers on the wall) and day lilies.

The main axis continues through a second yew arch and opens into a charming enclosed herb garden. The concept is used in its widest sense to include all sorts of plants that give scent. The garden's success lies in growing plants for every aspect and they combine together in a happy cottage garden miscellany.

A pollarded lime walk runs down to the east of the main court – morello cherries are trained on its wall with a solid stream of Spanish bluebells underneath to flower at the same time. At the final limes a cobbled path leads east under a long rose and wisteria pergola; the path is bordered with irises, *Lilium regale* and London Pride. At the far end a door through the north wall opens into an old orchard garden.

To walk through a door by the north-east corner of the manor is to enter an entirely different world. The splendid high north front of the house presides over a stone-balustrated terrace from which two flights of steps fall to a walled white garden. Aged espalier apples line the main walk and the eye is taken through gates at the bottom and up the opposite hill with its avenue of fastigiate elms. The white garden is full of good plants – notable are a couple of huge plants of the flat, highly scented *Daphne blagayana*.

Returning back up the slope another contrast is met with at the west front of the house; here a broad lawn stretches out enclosed by yew hedges appearing as venerable as the Manor itself (though this is a pose that often quite stripling yews adopt). At the end steps lead under an arch to the mount garden, a part of John Tradescant's original plan, its central high point crowned with the gnomon about which Hilaire Belloc wrote his famous, and dreadfully apt, couplet:

> *I am a sundial, and I make a botch*
> *Of what is done far better by a watch.*

Steps up to the south lead into the treed area of naturalised plants enlivened here with several standard amelanchiers – fleeting but charming. A low hedge of *Quercus ilex* separates garden from the meadows.

Outside the south-west corner of the main court a vast beech shelters colonies of *Cyclamen repandum* and *Anemone apennina*; by the house is a charming little box-patterned parterre full of pinks and spring bulbs. And here a door opens into the main south front courtyard of the house. The angled lodges are now ahead and the great cliff of worked stone behind provides a splendidly protected site. *Jasminum officinale* reaches to the machicolations on the roof, and *Magnolia grandiflora* has a site in keeping with its own scale. The floor of the court is an elegant composition of grass, cobbles and flags with four stone urns holding *Cupressus sempervirens stricta*. The mixed borders at either side are planned to give colour at all seasons from early bulbs to late herbaceous things; all are good.

Creech Grange

5 miles S of Wareham. Turn SW 1 mile S off the A357 Wareham–Swanage road.

The main drive drops through dark trees from the road (itself little more than a lane) to the stone gabled east front. Only a few urns of seasonal plants make any concession to the sombre scene of grey and green. A gap at the corner of the house leads to the lovely south front. Here all is light. A country Palladian façade looks serenely across its lawn to meadows which then rise steeply to the densely wooded Ridgway Hill. The great vista is canalised first by Irish yews in the garden, forest trees and a pair of urns in the field beyond and (a distant culmination) an arched and battlemented eye-catcher on the very top of the hill.

The west front of the Grange, closely hemmed in by trees, returns to an earlier style of architecture, draped with wisteria and clipped myrtle.

Here the water drops to a series of informal pools descending through the woodland. Rhododendrons and azaleas lighten the darkness in their season but cannot succeed in dispelling the pervading atmosphere of romantic gloom. There are plans for restoring this lovely landscape.

NOTEWORTHY SPECIMENS: *Liriodendron tulipifera* on south lawn.

Culeaze

7 miles NW of Wareham, 2 miles S of Bere Regis. From Bere take road to Wool, then second turn left; right at Tower.

The contemporary belt of high trees that surround the 1887 house give valuable protection to most areas of the garden; only to the south does the view open out to farmland and here a sunken garden provides a similar favoured site.

Along the east lawn is a broad shrub and herbaceous border in which euphorbias are a feature. Beyond are several interesting plants, notably a 13 ft high *Juniperus rigida* from Mexico. At this end of the lawn ten vertical junipers are planted in descending pairs and increasingly closely, which from the house gives a vista of false perspective closed by a small statue, this therefore appearing further off than in fact it is.

Through the wall is a traditional kitchen garden presided over by four huge vase-shaped apples. The main walk has standard wisterias and in the borders under the walls ornamentals juxtapose happily with trained soft fruit bushes. *Danae laurus* is grown on a commercial scale for cut foliage. The soil is an intractable acid clay.

Against the house is a glazed garden room with a huge mimosa pruned to form a canopy; *Jasminum polyanthum* clambers about vigorously.

NOTEWORTHY SPECIMENS: Judas Tree on east side, *Azara microphylla* to the north, Paulownia to left of drive.

Edmondsham House

1 mile S of Cranbourne, 3 miles NW of Verwood. On the B3081 from A354 Salisbury–Blandford Forum road.

Visitors enter at the west drive passing on the right a dell, once a large pond, now planted with trees and shrubs, and then sweeping round to approach the house. The view of its south west corner encompasses several centuries of English vernacular architecture; the sixteenth-century centre three storey porch flanked by seventeenth-century curly gables borrowed from the Dutch mode and the pedimented classical west front dating from the 1750s. The whole faces the little medieval village church.

The surrounding garden is a corresponding microcosm. Fine trees, indigenous and exotic (this is good tree country, a big *Sequoiadendron gigantea* dates only from 1906) sweep mixed borders with shrubs under-planted first with summer herbaceous material and then with spring bulbs. High brick walls enclose a series of kitchen gardens with wall fruit, herbaceous borders and traditionally grown vegetables.

At the end of the lawns that extend from the west front a small circular amphitheatre, enclosed and hidden by high trees, is known locally as a once-used cockpit. Nearby, of more botanical interest are large plants of *Syringa amurensis* — a tree-sized lilac from Siberia — and viburnum.

NOTEWORTHY SPECIMENS: Medlar north of house, *Juglans nigra*, *Magnolia acuminata* by the church, Mistletoe on limes.

Forde Abbey

4 miles SE of Chard and 7 miles W of Crewkerne. Well signposted off the A30. Twelfth-century Cistercian monastery also shown. May to September, Wednesdays, Sundays and Bank Holidays.

A long lime avenue from the entrance gates gives way to billowing yew hedges of great age and finally to the splendidly romantic south front of the Abbey; remarkably complete Cistercian buildings with seventeenth-century embellishments.

Ahead, on the same axis, is a long canal behind which ground rises with mature forest trees as a frame. The broad walk passes between a wall with interesting climbers and a wide herbaceous garden which borders the canal. Clipped Irish yews make architectural points and act as divisions in the border. Each section is planted with a different colour scheme.

At the canal's west end a woodland garden is reached with fine rhododendrons, magnolias (*M dawsoniana* is over 30 ft high — but its flowers are apt to be caught by late spring frosts to which the area is sadly subject), dogwoods and associated species. Ground cover plants are well used and there are good spreads of several hardy cyclamen; *C.repandum* with marbled leaves and spring flowers, *C.coum* and *C. hederifolium*. All seed themselves around and appear in unlikely spots.

Continuing to climb yet moving south the visitor gets the best view of the house below to the north-east. Across the west drive a lake comes into view; this is fed by three streams. All around are fine trees – often rare, such as *Fraxinus monophylla* and the southern beech, *Nothofagus obliqua*. Huge areas of naturalised bulbs make a brave show in spring.

At the top end of the lake an extensive bog garden contains lysichi-tums and rodgersias in quantity; candelabra primulas are a feature in May and June and an unusual large fern, *Blechnum tabulare* (*Lomaria megellanica*) flourishes by the cascade. In spring, too, are big patches of the hooded, purple and stemless flowers of *Lathraea clandestina*. This is an unusual parasite, related to the more common broomrapes, on the roots of poplars and willows. It seems to do no harm.

Returning now towards the Abbey (and still keeping a botanical weather eye open for surprising trees) the visitor is irresistibly drawn to an architectural garden house made, walls and roof and all, of living beech. This was planted in 1933 and it is worth noting how alternate short and tall plants compose the whole. A window to the south overlooks the lake and makes a perfect spot for observing the wildfowl while remaining unobserved oneself.

A path now leads eastwards along the top of the rise above the south front of the Abbey. Below lies the great expanse of golden stone while to the right across a ha-ha the main vista extends into parkland, the line now canalised by an avenue of black walnuts and limes. These were planted in 1937–8 and hence are not yet fully mature.

Continuing eastwards, a shallow dell-like area, known as the rock garden, is reached. Rocks exist but the scale of the trees and shrubs there (*Cornus macrophylla* and zelkova are particularly fine) is such that the term is hardly descriptive. An opening on the farther side leads into the arboretum begun in 1946. Many of the specimens have already reached forest-tree size and most have been pruned from a forestry point of view to encourage tall trunks and high crowns. From the arboretum one may drop down to the entrance drive at many points, depending on time availability and stamina. The keen plantsman of course will continue to the end though fearing, with reason, that he is bound to have missed something. There is, in fact, 1½ acres of kitchen garden and nursery still to be seen.

NOTEWORTHY SPECIMENS: Too many to list.

Hinton St Mary Manor

On the E side of Hinton St Mary village on the B3092. 2 miles N of Sturminster Newton, itself on A357 Blandford Forum–Sherbourne road.

Jacobean house and mediaeval church make a fine picture; to the left only a hedge of the old-fashioned 'Roseriae de l'Hay' separates garden from churchyard.

The south front of the house is cushioned into its site with billowing heaps of wisteria, *Euphorbia wulfenii* and *Abutilon vitifolium*. From here the full garden, apparently, is seen. To the left are shrub borders beyond which a gate leads to the orchard falling away eastwards. Ahead, across the valley of the Stour, are distant Bulbarrow Hill and Fontmell Down. Framing trees are venerable elms unlikely to survive the scourge of Dutch elm disease. The main vista travels along double mixed borders some fifty yards long, planted luxuriantly with shrub roses, peonies and strongly architectural plants such as variegated *Phormium tenax*. At the end young limes, presumably for pleaching, continue the line.

To the east hitherto unseen is a sunken pool garden formally planned and planted with Rose 'Iceberg', silver leaved plants and pinks. To the west, beyond a vast mediaeval tithe-barn a circular gazebo and great elms preside over a cool green garden which, virtually unplanted (apart from *Hydrangea petiolaris* on a wall) contrasts dramatically with the proceeding gardenesque.

NOTEWORTHY SPECIMEN: Weeping ash.

Hyde Crook

At Frampton, 5 miles NW of Dorchester on W side of A37 Dorchester–Yeovil road. 1 mile Yeovil side of Grimstone.

Hyde Crook must be one of Dorset's most surprising and rewarding gardens. The drive branches downhill from the busy Dorchester–

Yeovil road into thick woodland. Having driven over miles of rolling chalk downland, immediate glimpses of rhododendron and camellia have an air of unreality. A first look should be given to the south front of the severe 1930's house where from a flagged terrace the ground drops down and away to the Hardy monument on Black Down above Abbotsbury.

On all three other sides high woodland encloses the ground, covered in their season with great swathes of aconites, snowdrops, narcissi, cyclamen (*C.repandum* and *C.neapolitanum*) and, of course, native primroses and bluebells.

A path westwards leads through the wood to a kitchen garden area with a pair of long herbaceous borders, redolent with chalk; at intervals in the enclosing hedges are standard wisterias, in both the usual and white flowered forms. By the greenhouses a 20 ft high many-stemmed mimosa (*Acacia decurrens dealbata*) takes full south-west exposure yet flowers well in February.

Returning to the wood a higher path leads eastwards above the house and gradually indigenous trees give way to exotics. Triads of *Acer griseum, Amelanchier canadensis*; a huge cercidiphyllum is encircled with parottias, the whole making a stunning effect in autumn. *Magnolia x veitchii* has reached 50 ft in height.

A once broad walk of Japanese cherries is met at right angles but the spread of growth has arched it over. Behind, *Viburnum tomentosum mariesii* has reached near-tree proportions.

Further on, suddenly, the flora changes for here a narrow strip of greensand makes possible the full range of calcifuge plants. All exist in quantity, except rhododendrons which were not much liked by the original planters in 1936. Instead emphasis is on enkianthus, styrax, magnolias (*M.campbellii* is over 40 ft high), acers, and camellias. The latter, including open-ground *C.reticulata* have made, in the rather heavy shade, beautifully diffuse plants covered in flower from March to May inclusive.

The cross walk at which these appear should be explored in both directions. Following it south the drive is met again across which a long magnolia avenue extends. Originally planted in pairs, occasional singles only remain but here are huge plants of several *M. x soulangiana* forms, *M.kobus, M.stellata* and large deciduous-leaved summer-flowering species *M.tripetala* and *M.officinalis*. A remarkable collection.

Returning back to the house along the drive one is impressed by the broad showering habit of numbers of *Prunus subhirtella*. Although this is clearly a spring garden interest is always provided by the diversity of material. It must be seen often.

Kingston Maurwood

1 mile E of Dorchester off the Dorchester–Puddletown road. Turn SE at Stinsford.

Few counties can be as fortunate as Dorset to have its Agricultural College based around *two* distinct great houses. The surroundings of both are used for teaching and demonstration gardens of all types.

Seen immediately is the classical cube in Portland Stone built in the early eighteenth century for the Pitts, and the gardens offer a range of styles from the Browneian landscape school to the present day.

It is perhaps best to progress backwards in time, for moving along the west front of the house balustraded terraces and formal topiary gardens date mainly from the 1920's. A first enclosed garden, once containing a pond, now planted, has secondary hedges of various hebes. *Clematis Armandii* 'Snowdrift' is on the far wall.

Moving round the southern side other enclosed garden rooms are found, some big, some small. From the highest a long vista leads the eye southwards through the clipped yews, and the huge oaks above the lake. Fortuitously it is now suitably closed, exactly on centre, by that most contemporary of eye-catchers – an electricity pylon some miles away.

Steps from the viewing point lead down to the red garden whose pool and garden-house are surrounded by *Prunus pissardii*, *Berberis thunbergii atropurpurea*, and stretching northwards a broad avenue of copper beech.

Steps to the south (the bank planted with Spanish gorse and *Genista lydia*) lead through an iris garden to a circle of high hedges with niches for now missing statues. This gives on to a pair of broad herbaceous borders on the grand country-house scale. Rambler roses are trained up tripods for height and weight. A cross vista to the left leads back through a rose garden to the main garden front of the house.

At the bottom of the borders a steep bank falls to a canal and through the trees to the lake. The bank is planted solidly with laurel and kept cut (once a year) at 3 ft high. Following along the top of the bank towards the house groups of shrubs, both new and old, add to the interest, and educational value, of the scene: a collection of modern lilacs, rhododendrons and azaleas in imported soil, specimen trees. Below the house a great *Cedrus libani* dominates the slope as it falls to the lake.

Areas of bulbs and an alpine meadow give early interest.

From the lake edge one moves east and the canal, having passed under the main slope, emerges to flow through an enclosed 'Japanese' garden of acers, primulas and associated species. The hardy palm *Trachycarpus fortunei* flowers well.

Continuing eastwards a garden temple in the Doric mode makes the point at which time changes, for on the rise the fine early seventeenth-century house stands. Behind it are further teaching gardens all of which offer much to the keen amateur. The manor field has been planted with a wide selection of trees for confined spaces – mainly fastigiate forms. Its walled garden has been divided again and again by hedges – all different for comparison – into some 30 demonstration areas varying from a 30 by 10 yard 'Royal Horticultural Society' vegetable garden (half now run on a no-digging system) to a plot to show salt-tolerant shrubs.

Greenhouses behind – including nearby a town courtyard with raised beds of alpines – show a similar range of plants and methods of cultivation.

Mapperton

2 miles SE of Beaminster. Turn S off the B3163, this being off the A356 Dorchester–Crewkerne road. Or, from S turn NE off the A3066 4 miles N of Bridport.

The drive follows the contour above a steep-sided north-south valley in which the principal garden lies. But first the entrance front of the sixteenth-century house with, at right angles, the associated classical stables (plus magnificent wisteria) and coach-house must be admired. A great walnut provides a centrepiece which the view passes westwards over a ha-ha to the open fields beyond.

From this delightful essay in the landscape school it is all the more surprising to pass to the north side of the house. Here a severe eighteenth-century façade looks over a level croquet lawn bordered on two sides by 15 ft walls. *Solanum jasminoides* flourishes as does a superb *Clianthus punicens* by a gazebo to the north east.

At this point another jump in time occurs – in fact two – both forward and back. Below is an involved 1920's pastiche of seventeenth-century formality; steps, terraces, topiary, waterworks. The steepness of the site made major constructional works necessary and all is on the grandest scale.

The top feature is now a golden Ham stone orangery built 1966–8 and from here views are obtained southwards along the entire valley. Moving down, a circular pool marks a cross vista, then a stone and wood pergola leads to a central garden-house built above a vast retaining wall. Some 20 ft below two rectangular pools succeed each other, the first for people the next for lilies and fish.

Above to the right Mapperton Manor hangs over its valley. To the left in a grove of tall Scots pines the garden develops a more informal character. Here are camellias and rhododendrons through which a path leads further down the glen. Quantities of *Gunnera manicata* mark the stream and the east bank is planted with young specimen trees and shrubs.

Eventually a group of ash trees is reached with added eucalyptus and other exotics which mark the end of the main valley garden; however, the visitor is led up the steep slopes to the southern side of an adjoining valley planted with broad swathes of trees and shrubs and eventually back to the house.

Melplash Court

On W side of A3066 midway between Bridport and Beaminster.

An avenue of limes leads to the entrance court, itself lined with shrub roses and shaded by cedars and groups of contrasting whitebeams and purple sycamore. A gate to the left leads to a broad croquet lawn with a huge old yew mushroom as a focal point.

To the right a raised border holds old-fashioned roses and other shrubs; behind a beech hedge to the left by a garden-house a path follows a tiny stream down past groups of camellias to the main valley which it meets at right angles.

At the south end of the croquet lawn steps descend to a grass terrace which overlooks the valley garden. Hence the cherries, sorbus and other trees can be both walked amongst or looked into at flower-level.

The low retaining wall between terrace and croquet lawn is clothed with *Hydrangea petiolaris* and its border is filled with *Lilium regale*. To the right a small pergola carries *Akebia quinata* and a yew cone is covered with the scarlet *Tropaeolum speciosum*.

Returning to the house, *Actinidia chinensis* has reached to the second floor and *Abutilon megapotamicum* succeeds well. Round the corner beyond a huge deodar is pomegranate and the self-clinging *Campsis radicans*.

West of the house the garden merges with farm buildings; a herb garden of chequerboard flags abuts the circular, inhabited, dovecote. Behind a thatched woodshed a hedge of *Rosa rubrifolia* conceals a garden shelter and a collection of peonies. From this seat a view is obtained down the valley which eventually, through informal plantings of trees and shrubs, ends in a lake.

Minterne

Cerne Abbas, midway between Dorchester and Sherbourne, 3 miles N of Cerne Abbas on the old A352.

It must be stated at once, for the benefit of those whose minds dwell morbidly on 'ponticum' and switch off at the word, that Minterne has been famous for its rhododendrons since the Hooker species were planted here nearly a century ago. Yet in spite of their predominance this is no rhododendron garden in the arid, restrictive use of that term. Indeed the lushness of all growth makes such a thought impossible.

From the east front of the great 1900's house the lawns slope steeply to a lake with archetypal English parkland flowing up beyond. The cows appear as perfectly posed as the trees. So it is not easy to accept that this is entirely a product of eighteenth-century land-scaping, the difficulties of which are recalled by Admiral Digby's words (he had bought the estate from Charles Churchill, brother of the first Duke of Marlborough) on visiting the plantations on the bare hills, 'mostly dying except beech'. Yet eventual success made possible the woodland gardening of the last 100 years.

This is equally remarkable. South of the house, beyond wide lawns and across a sunken track is a wood following the shape of a huge horseshoe. Entering one arm eventually brings you out at the other. But it is not as simple as that. The eastern arm drops down following the outflow of the lake; this is first canal-like, then it becomes a stream bordered with water and bog plants. Inside the wood the ground is near-precipitous to the right with intersecting paths up and down the slope. All around are trees and shrubs remarkable for their size. This should not surprise as to Minterne came material from most of the important plant collectors of this century; Wilson in China in 1903 and 1906 and Rock, Forrest, Farrer and Kingdon-Ward between the wars.

Towards the bottom of the valley divisions of the stream are crossed and recrossed with little bridges. Every path should be explored for every turn brings fresh excitements; a grove of *Trachycarpus fortunei* whose hairy trunks are like the legs of many monstrous mastodons, Japanese maples which have reached real tree size, cercidiphyllum, as lovely in spring as it is spectacular in autumn. Such size of woody growth is matched by equally generous ground cover – trachystemon, gunnera and petasites. Arching bamboos emphasise the Eastern flavour.

All this greenness cools the brighter rhododendron admirably and helping too are generous plantings of *Rhododendron luteum* (the common but unsurpassed yellow azalea). Aficionados of the genus will note the tender species and hybrids such as 'Lady Alice Fitzwilliam', many large-leaved types in surroundings that are entirely to scale and interesting hybrids made here such as *R. x* 'cinnkeys' (*cinnabarinum x keysii*) with red and yellow Desfontainea-like flowers.

Eventually paths move upward to curve round the western arm of the horseshoe through bluebell woods haunted by the bitter-sweet smell of wild garlic.

NOTEWORTHY SPECIMENS: *Davidia involucrata, Sequoia sempervirens, Juniperus recurva coxii, Magnolia obovata.*

Moigne Combe

6 miles E of Dorchester. Turn N off A352 Dorchester–Wareham road to Owermoigne. Through village and on for 1½ miles. House is W of road.

A long drive leads through woodland to the north front of the red-brick 1900's house. From the forecourt a gate to the right leads to a broad gravelled terrace which runs the west and south sides of the house. From the latter the position on its Bagshot Sands ridge can be better appreciated; through high trees the ground drops away across meadows to a lake in the valley after which there is further woodland to high Dorset chalk downs beyond.

West of the terrace, protected by trees, new plantings of rhododendrons extend to the present boundary (plans have been made to develop further here) and a view opens southwards down the slope. Some yards down leading back to the south terrace, a path is lined with *Enkianthus campanulatus*. Considering how delicately attractive the veined flowers are in spring and how dramatic its autumn colour it is surprising this ericaceous plant is not used more. Here it does well and seeds itself about.

Below, a belt path follows the meadow boundary. Directly under the house a complicated series of amphitheatrical rock banks are newly planted with azaleas; tree heathers succeed enviably with *Erica lusitanica* and *E.erigene* (*mediterranea*) seeding themselves around. From here are fine views of the lake.

Climbing the slope in a north east direction a pergola under the main terrace is reached. To give an extended season of interest it is planted with trained laburnum, and wisteria while clematis twines between the two. A low hedge of *Pittosporum tenuifolium* (which at Moigne Combe clips beautifully) edges the walk. Below is an amusing Edwardian conceit; a huge heart and lovers' knot outlined in stone and originally filled with seasonal bedding; this has now given place to lavenders and dwarf euonymus.

Further east camellias cluster around a gate into a high Scots pine wood. Unusually this is the home of innumerable rooks whose comforting cawing sounds everywhere. At the end of the wood an abrupt turn right gives onto a broad azalea-lined walk down the slope to the lake several hundred yards away across the meadow.

The waterside is closely planted with trees whose shapes, textures and colours contrast admirably; the light birch and swamp cypress with dark cedars and sequoias. Two big specimens of the latter are recorded as having been planted from pots in 1856 and hence must be amongst the oldest in the country. (The first seed reached England in 1843.) A walk circles the lake passing a bridge to a tree-clad island from which views open back to the house on its ridge to the north.

NOTEWORTHY SPECIMENS: *Pinus radiata* and *Pinus nigra* on garden front of the house.

Owermoigne Moor

6 miles E of Dorchester. Turn N off A352 Dorchester—Wareham road at Owermoigne. Continue through village. Owermoigne Moor after 2 miles at road fork.

Approaching the 1920's house from the road, through pines and silver birches, rhododendrons and heathers, there is a sudden aura of Sunningdale or Windlesham; Bagshot Sand and golf-course country. A wicket gate to the right of the gravel sweep gives entry to the garden proper, and the eye is immediately taken by a splendid gum tree — probably *Eucalyptus dalrympleana* — straight as a die and 50 ft tall.

Following the side of the house is a paved formal garden (once planted with roses which now have to be eschewed having been accepted as a favourite food of feral roe deer. These are brave enough hereabouts to peer in at the windows — doubtless to watch television programmes about deer). The beds surrounding a small pool are now planted with Mediterranean maquis species — lavenders, cistus, santolina with the lovely South African wand-flower, *Dierama pulcherrima* pushing through.

At the house-corner is a loggia overhanging the steeply terraced garden. The view drops down through carefully grouped trees (note a huge *Cupressus macrocarpa* draped in wisteria) to meadows, a glimpse of water, woodland, then up and away to chalk ridges and a feeling of the sea beyond. Every trace of Surrey suburbia is dispelled.

Eight steps down from the loggia is a broad terrace extending the width of both house and formal garden making a dry promenade to view the scene below. Here are sprawling plants of *Othonopsis cheirifolia* with its spatula-shaped near-blue leaves and cheerful yellow daisies and a good true-blue rosemary. *Libertia ixioides* and *Erigeron mucronatus* seed in the gaps between the flags. Behind, the house holds *Magnolia grandiflora*, passion flower and variegated euonymus.

It takes 20 more steps in three flights to reach lawn level and the huge bank thus constructed is generously planted with a range of hebes, pittosporums and other shrubs. A very large *Cistus laurifolius* is as good out of flower for its leaves as when starred with white in early summer.

The broad level lawn (in which patches of seedling *Calluna vulgaris* make an agreeable turf) is surrounded by plantings of trees, shrubs and lesser things. At the end where the ground drops again to the meadows is a collection of heathers and amongst a clump of pines spring bulbs in rough grass. To the right a big *Genista virgata* makes, when in flower in June, a splendid pair with the nearby blue-leaved *Eucalyptus gunnii*. The border on this west side of the lawn again has interesting shrubs – *Robinia kelseyi* with pink flowers and bristly pods, cornus species and so on. Ground cover includes hellebores, epimediums, *Alchemilla mollis* and galeobdolon. At its top a fine group of yuccas underplanted with bergenia makes a striking pattern of texture and shape.

This border gives on to a rectangular lawn dominated at its southern end by a very large *Cornus mas*. This is covered in yellow flowers in February. Borders here hold summer flowers and, under apple trees, a collection of day lilies. The ground drifts away westwards into woodland with calcifuge plants under the indigenous canopy. After the great drought of 1976 *Gaultheria shallon* remained cheerful and unscathed when all around rhododendrons were clearly in extremis.

Return to the house may be by the terraces or via various paths up the bank leading back to the formal garden level. Here are further good shrubs underplanted with bulbs and corms; *Cyclamen hederifolium* (*neapolitanum*) seeds itself about everywhere. The interest at Owermoigne Moor is well maintained at all seasons.

NOTEWORTHY SPECIMENS: *Eucalyptus dalrynpleana, Betula pendula* (north west corner of lawn).

Rempstone Hall

From A357 Wareham–Swanage road turn east, under railway bridge, opposite Corfe Castle. Proceed on the B3351 for 3 miles.

The main garden occupies a long rectangular shelf of two or three acres sloping gently away from the back (north side) of the house. Above to the west is a broad shelter belt of mature Scots pines – some 200 years old – and oaks. To the east ground falls again to meadows.

Against the house is a flagged courtyard from which a path, passing a swimming pool (effectively heated by solar panels that can just be discerned on the house-roof) bisects the garden. Beyond specimen trees on the left a clipped beech roundel encloses stone seats and formal beds.

To the right a small stream emerges from under the house and its route is marked by clumps of Libertia, whose starry white flowers above grassy leaves are good for a long season. Below, the stream is dammed to form a small lake (or large pond) with an island reached by a bridge. Architectural-leaved waterside plants such as *Peltiphyllum peltatum*, *Osmunda regalis* (the royal fern), irises and pampas grass combine in masses to give a fine effect. Gunnera fruits abundantly. A small swamp cypress (*Taxodium distichum*) is expected, no doubt, to replace old specimens elsewhere in the garden. One, now in its prime, is by the kitchen garden door. This garden, incidentally, should be viewed in autumn when hundreds of spikes of the lovely pink *Amaryllis bella-donna* are in flower against a greenhouse wall.

Beyond the lake, water can be heard falling until it is joined by the regular thud of a small ram-pump pumping spring-water by its own power to a higher level. This simple mechanism is worth seeing. From the ram-house paths lead back to the Hall via a big shrub border on the east and, to the west, steps by a disapproving marble bust rise to a woodland walk in the shelter-belt. From this path after a few yards another route by a domed stone garden-house enters a small formal rose garden and below an old rock garden conceived on the grand scale; many of its plants have grown to match and tree heathers in particular seed themselves around with abandon.

The front of the house supports wisteria, *Magnolia grandiflora* and a big bottle-brush (*Callistemon sp*).

Slape Manor

Netherbury, 2 miles S of Beaminster. Turn W off the A3056 Beaminster–Bridport road.

The entrance front of Slape Manor, facing north, is shaded by huge trees, notably a vast purple beech, and such trees are a main feature of the garden as one moves round. The small terrace at the south west corner of the house is the place from which to see this perspective panorama down the valley of the little River Brit; rounded beeches and limes, sharper conifers, with for added contrast, rhododendrons to the right and fine formal hedges to the left.

On the house at this point is a large *Campsis radicans* which, unusually for England, does flower well. *Buddleia colvilei* on the broad raised terrace between the wings is similarly obliging; so often these two plants are not. Continuing eastwards along the garden front a yew arch is entered and one is in a garden room made entirely of plants; the high hedges, a circular pergola on eight piers draped with wisteria and the house wall covered with *Rosa banksiae* – the double yellow buttons of which complement the wisteria's soft lavender perfectly.

Following the Lawson cypress hedge into the garden another such room is reached, a canal planted with water lilies surrounded by paving and two hedges of beech and yew, the one inside the other. A most satisfactory architectural effect.

From here a path leads across a small stream and then on the side of the valley to a woodland garden that winds back to the house on its west side.

NOTEWORTHY SPECIMENS: *Styrax japonica, Magnolia wilsonii, Platanus x acerifolia* in the field across the road.

Smedmore

Kimmeridge 7 miles S of Wareham. From the A351 Wareham–Swanage road turn W just N of Corfe Castle to Church Knowle. Follow signs to Kimmeridge.

Dramatic views of cliffs and sea are obtained from the approach to Smedmore. Its own road branches left from that leading to Kimmeridge Bay and ahead, between two huge conifers (one is Monterey pine, the other Monterey cypress – a good Californian pair), lies the house of fine local stone.

For the very necessary reasons of shelter (the sea is not only in sight but in sound) the gardens are behind the house with protective layers of conifers, holm oak and walling. From the car park at the rear a flight of steps drops to a flagged courtyard from which lead two small gardens. The second, with a broad flagged path, boasts a fine standard peach tree and several good wall plants.

An iron gate leads to the main classical south front of the house where a raised terrace above the lawn provides a home for South

African daisies and other composites that like the sun. The house carries a fine wisteria, a free growing *Clianthus punicens* and, on the adjoining garden-house, a splendid plant of the yellow, late-flowering *Clematis tangutica*.

Below the lawn three pairs of clipped bays linked by a rose screen give access to a wide mixed border and, beyond, a wilderness (using the term in its seventeenth-century, not perjorative, sense). Here are huge fuchsias, perhaps 15 ft high, *Parottia persica*, a cut-leaved lime and, in front of enormous yew trees, against which they show up so well, several big trees of *Prunus avium*.

A gate in the east wall gives access to a further walled garden used for vegetables, fruit and cut flowers.

NOTEWORTHY SPECIMENS: *Tilia cordata laciniata*, *Quercus ilex*, mulberry in kitchen garden, chimonanthus on inside of west wall.

Tarrant Rushton House

4 miles E of Blandford Forum. Take Witchampton road E from Blandford Forum or S from A354 at Tarrant Hinton. House below church.

The garden at Tarrant Rushton slopes strongly westwards with the little River Tarrant as its boundary. Only a long border above a 3 ft high retaining wall is above the entrance drive at the top end. Here shrubs and interesting herbaceous plants tumble profusely together (*Helleborus corsicus* grown like this is a revelation). Chalk is so near the surface that not only do calcifuge things have completely to be abjured but sequestrene has to be in frequent use to avoid chlorosis and death of relatively accepting plants.

A huge horse chestnut shades the south west side of the house and at its foot aconites, cyclamen and bulbous species grow; here and in other such shady places further cyclamen and hepaticas seed themselves around.

Below the west front of the house a narrow border holds a quantity of *Dictamnus albus* and this warm spot is ideal for the burning bush to perform its party trick on a balmy evening.

A high wall divides the area below providing protective backing for both a north and a south border. On the north, amongst other things a big *Hydrangea petiolaris* is enlivened by Clematis 'Perle d'Azur' clambering through it. Nearby, surprisingly, *Cardiocrinum giganteum* succeeds. At the bottom watch should be kept for the sky-blue pea flowers of the Himalayan *Parochetus communis* poking above its clover-like growth: clearly this charming little plant is much hardier than generally supposed.

Here is a gate through the wall leading to the south side. This is mainly a peony and delphinium border, with interesting climbers on the wall. The so-called evergreen laburnum *Piptanthus nepalensis* does well.

Following the contour above the impeccable box-edged kitchen garden a west-facing border below another retaining wall contains young shrubs and a wide collection of bulbs to give interest over a long period. A second arch gives on to a further kitchen garden and elegant fruit cage. Grown so well, produce for the table becomes a legitimate part of the garden scene, not to be hidden away. Perhaps here a magnificent old espalier 'Winter Nelis' pear on the stable wall has shown the way.

Warmwell House

6 miles SE of Dorchester. Turn off N from A352 Dorchester–Wareham road towards Warmwell village.

The drive, past iron-railed paddocks, sweeps up to the apparently semicircular front of the fine stone house. However, the curved effect is caused by a flat central part with canted wings and this unusual arrangement is a refronting of around 1620. Ahead a broad lawn leads, with no sign of the hence very effective ha-ha, to meadows in which foals graze. Great trees frame the view.

To the left ground rises steeply and into the slope a square lawn has been cut (this in the early years of the century). A central walk with a small pool leads to a flight of steps rising to the top of the high retaining wall. Beyond paths lead from grass into mature beech woodland with recent underplanting of rhododendrons and azaleas.

Similar steps rise on the other two sides and the formal lawn and the borders which are thus bisected have newly been put down to low shrubs and long-lived herbaceous subjects such as peonies.

Further north, behind the house, two walled gardens display both vegetables and flowers and in an upper area a fine *Rosa rugosa* hedge conceals a swimming pool. A long south wall for peaches and other dessert fruit still has its traditional glazed lean-to roof. Glasshouses grow vines, figs and cut flowers for the house.

NOTEWORTHY SPECIMEN: *Pinus radiata*.

Waterston Manor

Lower Waterston, 5 miles NE of Dorchester. Turn NW off the A354 Dorchester—Blandford Forum road at 'Blue Vinney', Puddletown, on to the B3142 and on for 1 mile.

The villages around Puddletown both in name and atmosphere inevitably recall Thomas Hardy. So it is right that Waterston Manor is the original of Weatherbury Farm (Batsheba Everdene's bower) in Hardy's *Far From the Madding Crowd*. From under an arch the gravel drive sweeps up before a Virginia-creeper covered west front. Behind a wall can be glimpsed a highly productive orchard, but the main garden is behind the house. This is approached from the south where an west-east pollarded lime walk divides three small formal gardens from the large lawn against the splendid 1600's east front of the house.

From the central three storey porch, with its naively primitive Renaissance decoration, steps descend to a long, very narrow canal edged with pinks and rock-roses. The vista is closed by a huge copper beech.

Behind the beech a path can be found to take one north beyond the hedges that border the East Garden. Better, however, is to use the little wrought-iron gate by the house. Here ground from the pillared north front rises gradually to the road. The formality of this sombre aspect is entirely successful; four big Irish yews, a central roundel and glimpses to one side of a seat through old yew hedges by a garden-house and opposite a green vista to the park beyond.

NOTEWORTHY SPECIMENS: *Mahonia japonica* in deep shade, *Carpenteria californica* on west front.

WATERSTON MANOR

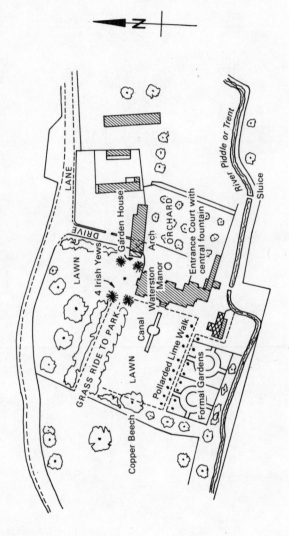

The Gardens of Hampshire

Ashford Gardens

2 miles N of Petersfield, off Alresford road (B2146). Turn right 400 yards past Cricketers Inn.

The great garden of Ashford Chase, begun in the early years of this century and made justly famous by the first Lord Horder over many years, is in one of the most splendid positions of all Hampshire gardens; a deep valley with enormous hanging beech woods all around. The property is now separated into three units with the original house being divided into flats. Not surprisingly, therefore, maintenance of the vastly labour-intensive grounds that go with it is no longer perfect. This may be sad but the site and the splendid trees, both local and exotic make a visit well worth while.

From the house a wide grass terrace slopes gently away westwards, its vista being closed 250 yards away by the arch of a pool garden. To the left the ground falls steeply to the stream, a constant sound of water indicating the presence of a series of falls as yet out of sight.

All around mature trees and shrubs surprise by their size; *Davidia involucrata* (handkerchief tree), liriodendron (tulip tree), cercidiphyllum and *Hydrangea sargentiana* with huge velvet leaves. Acers here are matched by those of:

Berryfield whose small garden is in fact the original rose garden of Ashford Chase; here are two green *Acer palmatum* and a dozen purple ones, several of which approach 20 ft in height. People who are persuaded to plant this species in a tiny rock garden should be warned.

The 1820 garden front of Berryfield is worth noting for its use of local materials, blocks of clunch — a particularly hard chalk — with insets of sandstone in the mortar. The war poet Edward Thomas lived here and is commemorated by a plaque.

The furthest part of the original Chace garden is now around Old Ashford Manor. Here, using the fine inherited trees, new plantings are going forward.

From the south terrace, from which perfect lawns slope gently to the widened stream, a wide curving herbaceous border follows the contours round to the left. A 10 ft high clunch wall supports roses, vines, ceanothus and *Hydrangea petiolaris*. A pergola conceals the swimming pool.

The stream which bisects the garden is on four levels with falls and rock banks. On the far side the original 'hanger' is now planted with rhododendrons, azaleas and other calcifuges which succeed admirably in the humus of ages built up over the chalk. Series of logged steps wind to the top where a croquet lawn takes the place of the outdoor theatre which older visitors will remember (if only for the mosquitoes!).

NOTEWORTHY SPECIMENS: *Cercidiphyllum japonica* by the topmost pool — *vast* specimen with a dozen trunks, *Acer griseum* — flaking bark, *Eriobotrya japonica* (loquat) entrance front of house.

Ashton Cottage

1½ miles N of Bishops Waltham. Between the A333 and the B3035.

Ashton Cottage is found (eventually) in a narrow lane leading from Bishops Waltham to Curdridge. Both the cottage itself and its front garden are misleading; from the rear an immediate sense of space and also the remarkable planting become apparent. In 2 acres, with a part-time gardener, the owners have developed a plantsman's garden which holds, as well as a huge range of species, many ideas which smaller (and indeed bigger) gardens could well take up.

A paved terrace is dominated by a vast *Phormium tenax*, its sword-like leaves strong enough, but when exceeded by the flower spikes this is a remarkable plant indeed. Ashton Cottage possesses good rose and iris borders but it is the collections of shrubs that holds the interest.

Leaf textures and shapes (as with phormium) are important. *Mahonia japonica*, good at any season, combines well in summer with Aunt Eliza (*Antholyza paniculata*) and ligularia. A good border of grey foliage — *Artemesia arborescens* gets big — with a range of hostas also emphasises the foliage effect.

In the island shrub borders acers do particularly well; there is one for each season: *A.japonica* 'Senkaki' with red young twigs, *A.grosseri hersii* — a snakebark, *A.pseudoplatanus brilliantissimum*, remarkable in spring and *A.cappadocicum aureum*, brightly gold throughout summer.

Soil here is a heavy alkaline clay and to extend the range a large bed has been constructed with imported acid soil and raised with peat block retaining walls. Here primulas and meconopses flourish in the shade of calcifuge shrubs. Crinodendron has reached 12 ft and *Cornus florida rubra* flowers almost as well as in its U.S.A. home. Also good here is *Magnolia liliflora* 'nigra', which also obligingly put out the odd flowers for weeks after the main season is past.

NOTEWORTHY SPECIMENS: 16-year-old paulownia, ginkgo, *Yucca gloriosa*, *Stachyurus praecox*.

Bentworth Lodge

3½ miles NW of Alton, 9 miles S of Basingstoke on the A339.

Across wide farmed parkland the drive to Bentworth Lodge climbs gradually, eventually to sweep up to the 1870's house. Entrance to the garden is on the east side leading to a wide flagged terrace above a croquet lawn. On the house are fine specimens of *Hydrangea petiolaris* and the Moroccan broom, *Cytisus battandieri*. Although not climatically needing protection from frost this plant is grateful for wind shelter in such exposed positions. Soil is nearly neutral: a clay-with-flints cap over chalk.

Beyond, to the south, the garden extends in a series of parallels. A high yew hedge with topiary topping has shrubs to one side and a rose garden on the other dominated by a pergola of 18 pairs of piers built on the grand scale. This is clothed, apart from roses, with wisterias and clematis.

At the far end, a symmetrical small-leaved horse chestnut, one of the *Aesculus pavia* group, is backed by a bank of hydrangeas. Returning towards the house, behind herbaceous borders a warm wall on the west side shelters interesting plants — *Carpenteria californica*, *Salvia bethelii*, *Campsis radicans* and two contrasting clematis — *C.tangutica* and the evergreen *C armandii*.

Across the fields to the north a natural pond has been extended and its surroundings planted with rhododendrons, camellias and, for later interest, old-fashioned roses.

NOTEWORTHY SPECIMENS: Pair of *Cedrus deodara* on the main lawn.

Binsted Place

2½ miles NE of Alton and 4 miles SW of Farnham. From the Farnham–
Petersfield road (A325) turn off W at Binsted signpost by Bucks Horn Oak.

Whereas Kings Chantry looks west, Binsted Place at the other end of the
village has fine views to the south east to the heights around Hindhead
in adjoining Surrey.

The ground around this small sixteenth- to eighteenth-century
house has been recently replanned in terms of a series of small inter-
connecting gardens to give an illusion of space and surprise. Hence,
from the paved entrance courtyard one moves around the house into a
rose garden, a pond garden, the swimming-pool garden. The original
kitchen garden (note the collection of old chimney pots) is now half
young orchard. Through a wall is a lawn area on two levels with a
border of hydrangeas where another gate returns one to the drive.

None of these areas is of great size but a feeling of movement is
obtained by the divisions.

NOTEWORTHY SPECIMENS: Purple beech, Irish yews, golden and green.

Becksteddle House

7 miles S of Alton, E of the A32. Take the Petersfield road S of East Tisted,
then turn N towards Colemore (1 mile).

Described unashamedly by its owners as a do-it-yourself garden, this
acre and a half is a good example of sensible design and careful
maintenance related to the requirements of the household. Sport is
important hence grass on tennis court and croquet lawn is cared for.
The site, on the heights west of Selbourne, gets all winds that blow and
hedges – Leyland cypress by the drive and *Thuja plicata* (handsomer but
slower) as internal divisions are used in conjunction with walls to give
protection. The walls also are home-built but with entirely professional

finish.

To the right of the entrance drive is a small rhododendron garden in the shade of high ash trees. Beyond and opposite is the entrance to the garden proper. From the south terrace views open across farmland, framed by a curving herbaceous border and a broad band of shrubs. Having got well above its wall *Eucalyptus gunnii* defies the elements with impunity.

NOTEWORTHY SPECIMEN: *Prunus subhirtella autumnalis* on the main lawn.

Bohunt Manor

On the southern outskirts of Liphook. Turn W from the A3 just N of Crab and Lobster Inn.

Entering the garden through a small door to the left of the drive, the visitor moves from country lane and cornfield to broad lawns, specimen trees and the glint of water. A wide flagged terrace stretches the full length of the south front of the house at the foot of which *Romneya trichocalyx* and *Mirabilis jalapa* (Marvel of Peru) are very much at home. The latter, in defiance of convention, are not brought in for the winter and treated like dahlias (but then, at Bohunt, nor are dahlias!) and seem to do well.

The east-west line of the terrace continues down three steps in a long pair of herbaceous borders at the end of which the lake is framed by tall bronze storks. The method of support of the herbaceous plants, with stretches of commercial chrysanthemum wire plus wire uprights which can be raised at will, is worth noting. The lake and its wildfowl, native and exotic, are a major part of the raison d'être of this garden; their continual movement and occasional calls attract the attention at all times.

But good plants are not neglected. On walls of the kitchen garden behind the house are a pair of ceanothus almost 20 ft high and a fig fruits heavily. At their base are *Nerine bowdenii* and schizostylis for autumn interest. From here the visitor enters an area to the west of informal island beds of shrubs and ground cover plants where *Allium albopilosum* seeds itself around. The beds merge into an extensive shade and bog garden at the north east corner of the lake. Surprisingly, the duck and geese do not appear to interfere with the plantings of hostas, lilies, lysichitum and astilbes.

A path leads round the lake and continues on the south into the wood which makes so strong a backcloth to the scene. Here rhododendrons and azaleas succeed under mature Scots pines and indigenous oaks.

NOTEWORTHY SPECIMENS: *Liriodendron tulipifera* on south lawn — very large, *Betula pendula* south of lake — two huge specimens, *Robinia hispida, Actinidia kolomikta*, on west side of kitchen garden wall.

Bramdean Farmhouse

On main Winchester–Petersfield road (A272) 4 miles SE of Alresford. At the E end of Bramdean village.

Around the timbered house and old farm buildings the garden extends into what was originally the prerogative of the farm alone. Such extension offers a range of walls, aspects and opportunities; all are owner-maintained.

The drive sweeps between mixed borders, well planted, of shrubs, roses and herbaceous things. Interest continues for a long period; *Ligtu alstroemerias*, thus associated, become self-staking. Roses on walls invariably share their spot with a clematis; on a barn, for example, a pink 'Hagley Hybrid' clematis merges with 'Madame Gregoire Stachelin'.

West of the house, gravel is separated from lawn by a hedge of Hidcote lavender. A line of deciduous azaleas denotes no amelioration of the local chalky soil but an excavated area helped by sequestrene.

In front of the thuja hedge is a mainly white herbaceous border and beyond a swimming-pool garden. The otherwise flat site has been enlivened by using the spoil to make a raised terrace. The retaining wall sports aubrieta, helianthemums and other colourful spilling plants.

NOTEWORTHY SPECIMENS: *Acer pseudoplatanus* (sycamore).

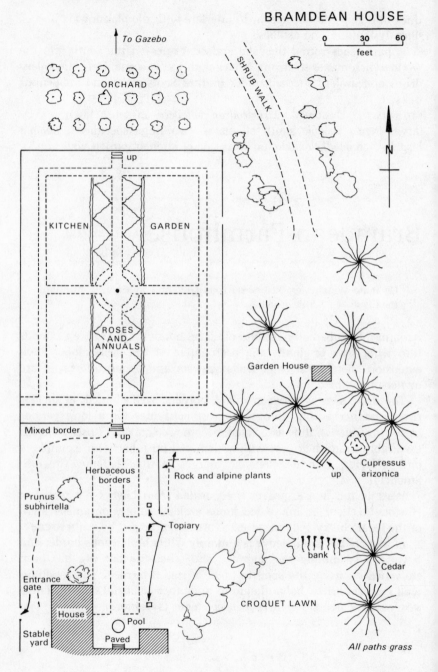

BRAMDEAN HOUSE

0   30   60
feet

To Gazebo

ORCHARD

SHRUB WALK

N

KITCHEN   GARDEN

ROSES
AND
ANNUALS

up

Garden House

Mixed border   up

Herbaceous
borders

Cupressus
arizonica

Rock and alpine plants   up

Prunus
subhirtella

Topiary

bank   Cedar

Entrance
gate

House

CROQUET LAWN

Stable
yard   Pool

Paved

All paths grass

Bramdean House

On main Winchester–Petersfield road (A272) 4 miles SE of Alresford. At W
end of Bramdean village.

The fast Petersfield–Winchester road that whirls cars through the little
valley village of Bramdean is also apt to rush them past one of the
consistently fine gardens of Hampshire; one where eclectic choice of
plants and felicity of grouping has been maintained since it was built
up to its present form by the late Mrs Feilden – herself county organiser
for the National Gardens Scheme for many years.

Great billowing hedges of mixed yew and box between pairs of
armorial gates half hide the Georgian south front of Bramdean House
from the road. The garden is virtually all at the rear and is entered by a
little door in the stable yard. The ground, a long slope to the north (and
hence facing south) still retains the basically simple outline of earlier
times; three square or rectangular gardens enclosed by brick walls and
hedges making perhaps 6 acres in all. An axial corridor cutting through
each divide provides a vista from the centre of the garden front of the
house to a cupola'ed gazebo some 300 yards away at the top.

Although the three gardens are linked with decorative features, in
each the prime ornamental area is naturally the lowest one against and
around the house. Here with a backdrop of mature beeches, limes and
cedars and a foil of lawn is a fine collection of herbaceous and shrubby
plants. Immediately outside the main door is a small circular pool from
which two wide herbaceous border lead up and away. The emphasis is
upon mid-summer interest but early bulbs and plants whose foliage
remains good after flowering extends the season in both directions.
Bocconia cordata, the lovely beige-pink plume poppy is used a lot, to be
seen and to be seen through into other things.

West of this herbaceous walk a lawn and its central *Prunus subhirtella* (enlivened in autumn with pink and white *Cyclamen hederifolium*) is
edged with mixed borders. Plants fill the ground, cover the walls and
spill forward in the gayest profusion; annuals are not neglected if by
their use the gap left by spring bulbs can offer interest at a later stage.
This sort of continuous attending to detail in addition to meticulous
maintenance lifts a garden into a very particular class. Staking, too,
with the use of brushwood, wire guards and tiny wattle hurdles is
impeccable; it has to be if a large number of plants is not to develop into

a muddle.

At the east side under a broad cedar is the croquet lawn, on a lower level and half-hidden from the rest by shrubs; a big horizontal juniper repeats the effect provided by the lowest branches of the cedar across this lawn. Interestingly a young deodar cedar planted no doubt to take the place of its mature relation when the latter eventually dies, is doing well in dense shade and apparent inevitable drought.

The axial walk leads into the second garden by a high wrought iron gate at the head of steps. Here is basically a classical kitchen garden, a 2-acre high-walled square with trained fruit – suitably chosen for each aspect – and the full range of vegetables. When well-grown, as here, vegetables can be immensely satisfying – in an aesthetic as well as the gourmand's culinary sense – but here the intentionally decorative interest is taken up through the main vista with wide borders of roses and annual plants. These are arranged in a chevron pattern, giving large triangles of each. At the central point where the cross-walks intersect, a circle of old yew hedging encloses a sundial. Other features are worth noting; small beds of lily of the valley for cutting; peonies at the base of the fruit cage for a similar purpose; solomon's seal and hellebores in a shady spot; rows of seedling foxgloves to take the place of those that have flowered (and hence finished) in the borders. No space is wasted; all is properly used and one gardener maintains the lot.

A second similar iron gate opens into the top garden which holds at its end the pretty cupola- and wind-vane-topped gazebo or apple house (with good plants of *Kolkwitzia amabilis* on its front). This area is really old orchard and displays a mass of daffodils and so on in spring; the rough-mown grass also holds a blue carpet of speedwell which acts as a delightful foil to the predominant yellow of spring.

Amongst the trees have been planted a range of shrubs and shrub-roses. More specimen plants of interest can be found in a walk leading south east on the outside of the kitchen garden wall; particularly noteworthy is a mature handkerchief tree, *Davidia involucrata*, not minding the chalk at all. This walk eventually emerges under the huge beeches above the croquet lawn in the bottom garden. Even more pleasurable, however, is to retrace steps down the main walk with the double filigree of gates opening to reveal the wide north front of the house and the rolling Hampshire Downs beyond.

Having noted, first perhaps, the broader effects of planting, the returning walk will reveal something of the components – common plants and rare plants, all good ones. Each will find favourites; blue agapanthus, black or green veratrums, herbaceous clematis, much grey foliage and bulbs in succession from snowdrop to colchicum. Each season offers its pleasures.

NOTEWORTHY SPECIMENS: *Davidia involucrata, Cupressus arizonica conica.*

Broadhatch House

In Bentley village midway between Alton and Farnham. Turn NW at village pond and bear right at fork.

Bentley, north east of Alton seems to collect gardeners. The climate is apt to be surprisingly extreme for Hampshire, and here at Broadhatch House the soil is an unkind clay; yet again there are lots of good things to see.

The $3\frac{1}{2}$ acres (tended by one man) spread from the east (entrance), south and west sides of the house. A spring garden holds acers, *Magnolia liliflora* 'nigra' and remarkably good plants of *Daphne* 'Somerset'. Beyond are mainly deciduous azaleas underplanted with bulbs and, for summer interest, *Lilium pardalinum*. This stately spotted turkscap is one lily that relishes the wet. An interesting evergreen in this south east corner is *Photinia fraseri* 'Red Robin' − the cultivar name referring to its spring shoots.

Moving west it is now possible to return towards the south front of the house through a rose garden of 'Peace' and hybrid musks or continue near the boundary through a collection of young acers and conifers. Liquidambar is doing well.

The house walls are well clothed. On the south is *Magnolia grandiflora*, the evergreen laburnum, *Piptanthus laburnifolius* and the charming little shrubby vetch *Dorycnium hirsutum* seeds itself around. Round the corner, planting in the West Courtyard is mainly grey, white and gold with one or two near-tender evergreens. Here grow myrtle, *Hebe speciosa* and the wavy-leaved *Pittosporum tenuifolium* − more usually seen in this area as cut foliage (from Cornwall) in florists' windows.

In part of an adjoining kitchen garden is the 'New' Rose Garden. Now over 12 years old there are billowing masses in a wide range of especially shrub and old-fashioned types. 'Fantin Latour' (*Centifolia*), 'Queen of Denmark' and 'William Lobb' (moss) are favourites. Grey foliage of senecio and artemesia complement. Nearby borders of peonies, delphinium and flag irises add their own particular seasonal pleasures.

NOTEWORTHY SPECIMEN: *Cupressus macrocarpa lutea.*

Broadlands

On S side of Romsey. Entrance lodge on A27 1½ miles from town centre.

Suiting its name perfectly, Broadlands is conceived entirely on the grand scale with wide views, and great trees; the epitome of the English Landscape school. Only the lawn on the south front, enclosed by topiary yew hedges is the obviously post Lancelot 'Capability' Brown addition.

The second Lord Palmerston employed in 1766 the duo of Henry Holland and Brown (the latter's father-in-law) to work on house and grounds respectively.

From the Ionic porticoed west front Brown's genius can be best seen. A smooth lawn drops to the sweep of the wide River Test flowing fast from the north; it then curves away and out of sight. This breathtaking view is framed by great trees – cedars, planes, beeches and limes – and continues up to a horizon of distant woods now punctuated by the tops of sequoias that Brown could not have known.

A down-river walk moves away south-westwards. Eventually at a bridge it leaves the waterside and returns eastward to give a view of the south front of the house with the fine classical orangery in the foreground.

Returning back towards the portico a small carrier of the Test emerges from under the great west lawn. A couple of hundred yards to the north it can be found to dive into the ground underneath an icehouse – providing no doubt both a cooling effect and drainage for the melting stored ice in a pre-refrigerator age. The carrier, with occasional falls, may now be followed upstream. It is bordered by huge planes and taxodiums and enters the pleasure grounds by a pretty garden-house overhanging the water. Here is a collection of magnolias and a halffallen liriodendron which makes the enjoyment of its usually distant 'tulips' more possible.

A flight of steps leads to the first of a series of walled kitchen gardens. In June *Wisteria multijuga alba* draping over a vinous-filigree bronzed gate makes a lovely picture, but although the walls and ground still provide fruit (the apple pergolas are notable) and vegetables, the available staff does not permit traditional maintenance of such labourintensive areas.

An inevitable question of visitors to historic landscapes concerns the age of this tree or that; answers usually have to be guessed at. Future visitors to Broadlands will be grateful at the numbers of commemorative trees, with dated plaques, planted by notable people over the last few decades. A particularly interesting group is of mulberries planted by Her Majesty The Queen and Prince Philip in 1957 to commemorate the 350th anniversary of the grant of Romsey's Royal Charter by King James I, who in 1607 also planted mulberries. All are now fruiting well in the middle kitchen garden lawn.

NOTEWORTHY SPECIMENS: Most forest trees, cedars, taxodiums.

Brockenhurst Park

S of Brockenhurst village on the A337. Turn E to old church. Drive is across lane to E.

Across the cattle grid the visitor drives through archetypal English parkland; some of the venerable oaks are as old as any in the country. Hence the surprise is all the greater on arrival in front of a modern brick house of unconventional design. It is emphasised by the entrance courtyard with its interesting wall plants – *Solanum crispum* and *Clematis montana* on the house itself, and a range of tender plants – purple prostanthera and scarlet callistemon for example – against the walls.

The visitor should then be blinkered as he moves to the garden front of the house to admire more lush wall and paving plants (*Clianthus puniceus*, the New Zealand lobster claw is a revelation when it does not have to be trained flat.) Only then should he turn to receive a second shock. For now, with the contemporary house behind, a grandiose Italianate garden extends ahead.

Gertrude Jekyll, writing in the first decade of this century, describes Brockenhurst Park as having more successfully assimilated the atmosphere of an Italian garden than any other place in England. And illustrations of the time show stonework, topiary and waterworks of daunting complexity.

The present owners, having replaced the remaining shell of the huge Victorian pile by a house suited to modern needs are gradually taming the wilderness that spread, after years of complete neglect, from the doors.

A broad canal runs north to south, with, like a post-Palladian stage-set, flights of steps and serried layers of plant growth developing from the formally clipped to billowing masses of trees beyond. Twenty topiary yews march the length of the canal and the whole rectangle is enclosed by hedges of sweet-bay (*Laurus nobilis*). These alone must be almost unique.

Having recovered from the shock and assimilated the view, it is now probably best to take a route outside the formal garden, to the west, and move uphill between it and the park under huge trees and through groups of shrubs. Some of the trees are remarkable; a vast deodar with 12 trunks (a forester's nightmare), many magnificent Lebanon cedars, five 200-year-old Scots pines, recorded as being amongst the first to be planted in the New Forest in modern times, and early (1850's) plantings of redwoods. On a smaller scale *Rhododendron decorum* is also from the first introductions to this country.

This open woodland garden looks outward to the park with the Forest falling away to the north and east in the distance, and inward through several cross vistas whose intersections are continually met. Vestiges remain, not only of the 1870's garden, but also of earlier designs, the whole a palimpsest which is still being worked upon, both in retrieving what is possible (and desirable) of the past and planting to provide for the future. Some 7 acres are cultivated.

NOTEWORTHY SPECIMENS: *Magnolia acuminata* (second biggest in Britain), *Quercus suber* (Cork oak), *Catalpa bignonioides*, *Kalopanax pictus* (Araliaceae, but confusingly like an acer).

Burgate Court

2 miles N of Fordingbridge on E side of the A338.

The garden at Burgate Court is sandwiched between the business of the A338 and the tranquillity of the Hampshire Avon. Fortunately a strip of kitchen garden and splendid holly, laurel and yew hedges only 25 years old (who says you have to wait a hundred?) completely insulate the one from the other.

Fine double hedge-backed herbaceous borders use red hot poker as exclamation marks which contrast with the white Californian tree-poppy, *Romneya coulteri*. Although the Avon is a classic chalk stream in its upper reaches, here it runs through flinty silt with a pH low enough for rhododendrons and camellias to succeed.

Passing these calcifuges and returning to the house one comes across two fine garden ornaments. In the rose garden a Renaissance (*c.*1500) wellhead and, as architrave to a yew arch, a splendid carved surround. This is of similar period and in detail resembles a bestiary with a Byzantine flavour.

Further walks border the river banks where the indigenous flora, as colourful as a border, is permitted to grow. A wooden bridge is draped with *Vitis coignetiae* and leads to an island packed with daffodils in their season.

NOTEWORTHY SPECIMENS: *Pinus nigra, Quercus ilex.*

Burley Grange

2 miles E of Burley village, itself 4 miles SE of Ringwood.

While the village of Burley claims to be the traditional centre of the New Forest, that centre was not, until recently, a particularly populous one. Most of the bigger houses are in a 1900's Jekyllesque (several in fact by Clough) style with tile-hung gables, casement windows and a wealth of old oak. The contrast of white walls, shallow grey-slated roof sash windows and general Regency restraint of Burley Grange is marked. Hence the simpler parts of its garden are the most successful. The entrance drive wheels in front of the house between great bastions of clipped *Rhododendron ponticum* some 20 ft high. This is, on such hungry acid soils, a splendid formal hedging plant – and still manages to flower quite well. To the left a large hammamelis and its relation *Parottia persica* should be noted.

On the garden front simple lawns take the eye to the open boundary fence and a view of typically open Forest.

A huge old wisteria clothes the loggia – both colour and texture, complementing the house most effectively.

A now well-grown *Magnolia kobus* was planted to commemorate the birth of a daughter of the house; this is a well chosen species for a charming idea; it will be coming nicely to flowering maturity as its owner comes of age. Hybrid rhododendrons surround a swimming pool, from which an informal walk leads along a border of hydrangeas and, surprisingly, acacias, through the walled kitchen garden back to the house-front.

NOTEWORTHY SPECIMENS: Oak by the pool (*Quercus robur*), *Cornus nuttallii*.

Calluna, 58 Merdon Avenue, Chandlers Ford

1 mile N of Chandlers Ford. Merdon Avenue leads W off old A33 Winchester–Southampton road.

This garden is the product of over 40 years keen plantsmanship and in about an acre of ground a vast array of plant species grow in remarkable profusion. The soil is typical New Forest acid loam.

The house is surrounded by a lawn and the grass in turn by a deep shrub border. This screen is pierced by narrow paths which, when entered, entirely give one the impression of being in a woodland garden of illimitable extent. Rhododendrons have reached the size expected only in the great gardens of the New Forest littoral – *R.cinnabarinum* is a dozen feet high, *R.loderi* rather more.

Below the shrubby material is a plethora of woodland floor species, erythroniums, trilliums, hellebores, trientalis and so on. In more open spots *Iris innominata* forms are a feature and colchicums give autumn interest. Not a corner is wasted.

Amongst particularly fine plants are a large *Styrax japonica* by the entrance gate and, further on a rounded *Eucryphia lucida* – a fine Tasmanian species, not often seen. Opposite on the house is the evergreen *Clematis armandii* through which *Abutilon megapotamicum* has scrambled 10 ft up.

However the most remarkable specimen in the garden is a huge *Camellia reticulata* 'Captain Rawes'. Originally planted to be trained on the garage wall it has made a vigorous tree some 20 ft high and with a trunk 18 in. round at 5 ft from the ground. This is worth a considerable journey to see at its best in a frost-free April, for without doubt it is the finest plant of its species – that I have seen – in three counties.

Melplash Court: the pond above the entrance front. The imposing gables are hiding behind a great yew

2   Formality with the spring display at Hinton Ampner House

3   The Apple House at the top of the orchard at Bramdean House closes the vista tha
    runs the length of the garden

CALLUNA

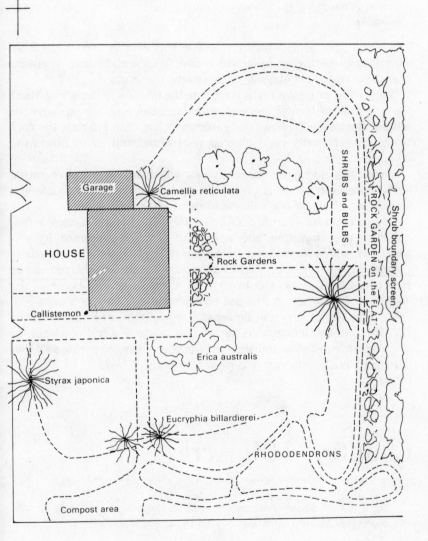

N

Garage

Camellia reticulata

SHRUBS and BULBS

ROCK GARDEN on the FLAT

Shrub boundary screen

HOUSE

Rock Gardens

Callistemon

Styrax japonica

Erica australis

Eucryphia billardierei

RHODODENDRONS

Compost area

Castle Top

Castle Hill Lane, Burley. N of village. Turn S from A31 Cadnam–Ringwood road at the Picket Post. Castle Hill Lane (rough gravel) on right as village begins.

The 'Castle' alongside which Castle Top was built in the 1900's is an early British earthwork from which fine views are obtained of distant open New Forest countryside of moor and woodland.

The garden dropping south west from the house is in two parts. There are a couple of formal terraces with mimosas and *Myrtus tarentina* against the house. Because the gardener is less than full-time the rock banks have recently been planted with cistus and other sun-loving labour-free plants.

Views are hidden by the high oak woodland. The native spring herbaceous layer is lovely; bluebells, stichwort, pimpernel, bugle and ferns to which lily of the valley and so on have been added.

Rhododendrons, of course, do splendidly; large-leaved *Grande* series, *cinnabarinums*, *augustinii* and a host of unusual unnamed hybrids which originated from the great garden of Borde Hill in Sussex where Colonel Stevenson Clarke produced *Camellia* 'Donation'. This too can be seen at Castle Top as is only right in a garden at the home of the daughter of its raiser. A fine red rhododendron is named 'Castle Top' and is a half-brother – and flowered first – of the better known 'Tally Ho'. This is not an immaculate garden, but one in which rhododendrons are seen uncrowded in uncontrived situations, similar perhaps to that of their native Himalayas. It is rather beautiful.

Chantry, 100 Acres

Off A333 Wickham–Portsmouth road, $2\frac{1}{2}$ miles E of Wickham church. Signposted to 100 Acres. Chantry on right, $\frac{3}{4}$ mile.

When an owner describes the soil of his or her garden as 'benign' it tells something not only of the medium itself but also of the way it is worked with – as distinct from being worked against.

Here on light, stony, acidic soil continually enriched with leaf mould grows a happy profusion of azaleas, roses, lilies; herbaceous things and shrubs juxtapose and spill about in what, clearly, must be seen as a somewhat sophisticated cottage garden in a wood.

A steep short drive leads up to the north side of the house. Against the road are two large geans (wild cherries: Housman's 'loveliest of trees'), good in flower, fruit and autumn colour. To the right of the slope is a big '*williamsii*' camellia with very small narrow leaves. Others appear around the garden and are seedlings from Caerhays in Cornwall, the home of this invaluable grex. By the house are, for comparison, conventional *Camellia japonica* forms. Opposite is a group of conifers where Lawson's cypress, ferny hemlock, fuzzy *Cryptomeria japonica elegans* compose, with showering bamboos, an interesting group.

The main garden is south of the shingled house. Informal terraces and lawns on several levels drop away into trees with distant views of the chalk scarp of Portsdown. Nelson's Monument above Portchester shows up as a pointing finger. Although in this colourful garden there is much to take the eye, at all seasons the visual centrepiece is a fine *Eucalyptus gunnii*. This is only 10 years old but flowers and fruits well and gives every appearance of maturity.

Beyond the centre lawn an avenue of cherries and wisterias pruned as bushes is underplanted with peonies, heathers and spurges. To the left a paved path leads down through a prodigality of species; *Meconopsis betonicifolia* succeeds in full sun and masses of *Lilium tigrinum* miraculously show no sign of virus disease. This path skirts the big gum and enters a wild area of apparently indigenous plants – pines, birches, heather. On a sheltered south west slope is bottle-brush corner where scarlet callistemons flourish and flower in July. The way leads back to the top of the garden at its north western point. Returning to the house two very white gums are emphasised by *Senecio leucostachys* at their feet.

Against the house is *Fremontodendron californica*, passion flower and roses, notably 'Aloha' – obviously a local favourite. Here, and by the side of a small greenhouse *Alstroemeria* 'Ligtu hybrids' in their astonishing range of colours behave as if they were illustrating their own seed packet.

Chilland

Martyr Worthy, 4 miles NE of Winchester, $\frac{1}{2}$ mile W of Itchen Abbas. Signposted 'Chilland' leading S from B3047.

One of the marks of the really successful garden is to know when to stop. What a temptation it is to all keen plantsmen to extend, as long as ground is available, areas of cultivation and the collections of plants within them. Frequently garden, not gardener, becomes the master and all time away is taken as it were surreptitiously. At Chilland a satisfactory balance seems to have been struck and in doing so a most satisfactory garden evolved, of interest to casual viewer and specialist alike.

Entrance is by a dark and rather unprepossessing drive but as soon as the house appears (good, Regency) so do interesting plants. Throughout the garden their association is the product of much thought, much trial and presumably even error (the two usually go together). Few areas are allowed to have only one season of display hence attraction is frequently both sequential and stratified.

An immediate example exists at the sweep before the house (this carries yellow and red fruited pyracanthas) where the small apple *Malus transitoria* is underplanted with *Tulipa orphanidea* to accompany the spring flower and *Cyclamen hederifolium* the autumn fruit. Left of the porch grows *Clematis alpina* 'Frances Rivis' – by far the best of the group.

The main garden area is now at hand. From the south front ground slopes gently to the River Itchen, its course marked by meadowsweet and rushes, then rises again on the other side to a low tree-covered hill. No exotic gardening competes with this gentle scene – the grass is first mown then rough-cut – except one vast, and surprisingly narrow, London plane, as old as the house and quite part of the place. To the left *Magnolia x veitchii* and a few rhododendrons share an area of prepared soil; to the right an exactly laid York stone path leads round to the west.

Borders and walls of the house combine to offer sites to a wide range of good plants. On the south is *Abutilon vitifolium*, several hebes, *Magnolia grandiflora* through which the brittle-stemmed grey *Senecio leucostachys* has climbed to reach first floor level. From the corner a diagonal vista aligns through groups of shrubs to the river meadows and cornfields. Beyond is *Buddleia crispa* from North India, good in leaf and flower, and further round winter sweet and *Stachyurus praecox* make a fine winter pair. Turning to the west front a wide ride leads ahead ending in a yew-hedge apse broken by central wrought-iron gates. On the right, linking with the flagged path that here has taken on a terrace role, a rectangular pool is set in further flags. It is backed on two sides by a wide raised bed full of good bulbs and corms. Big clumps of *Haberlea sp.* and other damp-impatient alpines flourish on the vertical sides. The prostrate *Daphne blagayana* makes a fine plant and here is a couple of feet nearer the nose than usual for its exquisite scent to be enjoyed. In summer *Tropaealum polyphyllum* tumbles from between the stones and although Chilland is not a warm garden *Euphorbia mellifera* seeds itself about. Opposite, mention must be made of a huge yew which has been cut back almost to a telegraph pole but which shoots into growth to form a cypress-like column up which rose 'Bobby James' has climbed. A good way of dealing with a plant which threatened to darken every aspect. Moving along the ride a broad tree-backed herbaceous border marches to the right and, to the left, several intercommunicating areas in which Chilland's best plant associations are seen. At the apse, openings right and left lead to tennis court and swimming pool respectively, both out of sight from the main walks. Turning to the mixed borders at a broad hybrid oak – perhaps a Turkey – there is much to see; roses and especially clematis climb about. Hence clematis 'Royal Velour' clambers over purple *Cotinus coggygria atropurpurea* and grey *Buddleia fallowiana*; even the description sounds good – the visual effect is even better. *Magnolia stellata* (with a little peat bed for Erythroniums in front) supports *C alpina*. Underneath the shrubs are hellebores, peonies and other herbaceous things which offer good leaves to supplement their flowers.

Steps to the swimming-pool garden also lead to areas of lilies; and here the little *Gladiolus colvillei* 'The Bride' is treated, and behaves, as if it were hardy.

Groups of shrubs – all underplanted with bulbs – to the south are grouped for foliage and autumn colour effect. Nerines are a feature and planted to grow through Jackman's form of rue; the October effect is outstanding. A particularly good group fronts a mulberry which is contemporary with the house and combines grey sea buckthorn, cornus, berberis, cotinus and variegated privet amongst others; it is worth standing back to see.

Several of the young specimen trees have reached a decent size in their 30 years or so. *Betula mandschurica*, the vertical *Malus tschonoskii*, Liquidambar and *Prunus sargentii* all add their flower or autumn colour or bark and help to make Chilland a garden to linger in.

Chilworth Manor

On A27 Southampton–Romsey road 1 mile NW of its junction with the A33. Signposted from 'Clump' inn.

As a hall of residence for Southampton University it is not to be expected that the grounds of this huge marine villa, stranded on high ground away from its Solent shore, can be impeccably maintained. Yet it has fine trees and shrubs and interesting aspects of design make a visit worthwhile.

The drive passes between a pair of thatched beehive-shaped lodges to an informal avenue of sequoias and other conifers. Sweeping up to the house it is bordered by standard rhododendrons. But the main grounds are on the other side of the house. Terraces fall to the west. To the left is an enclosed formal garden with a loggia supported by Baroque barley-sugar pillars. From here a narrow walk is edged by rhododendrons (mainly old hardy hybrids); both the usual mauve and uncommon white wisteria clothe the opposite wall.

One is brought below the main terrace to view the long vista framed between Ionic columns and a walk of deciduous azaleas. Resisting the temptation to follow this line it is wise to proceed across the garden front of the house shaded by a huge cedar. To the north west, below a meadow recently planted with cherries and bulbs, is a small lake with a rustic boathouse and good Taxodiums. Passing the lake it is possible to join the azalea walk at its foot. (A 30 ft broadleaved evergreen here is the unusual Californian laurel, *Umbellularia californica*, a few sniffs of whose bruised leaves is reputed to bring on dire headaches.)

A circular planting of high *Thuja plicata* is known as the deer ring and may be entered – a silent, shaded place. Leaving it a walk curves north-eastward towards the house following a virtual hedge of *Rhododendron amoenum* – spectacular in flower – and good specimen trees. Many are indigenous and the University Department of Botany is using the area for ecological studies.

NOTEWORTHY SPECIMENS: *Sciadopitys verticillata* (Japanese umbrella pine), *Chamaecyparis pisifera filifera*, *Arbutus unedo*, *Liquidambar styraciflua*, *Magnolia grandiflora*.

Cliddesdon Down House

1 mile S of Basingstoke in centre of Cliddesdon village on the B3046, across road from village pond.

When complaints are made about motorways' despoliation effect upon the countryside their occasional but none the less invaluable insulatory effects in limiting urban sprawl should perhaps be remembered with gratitude. The M3 at Basingstoke is a fine example; on one side housing estates as far as the eye can see; on the other untouched Hampshire downland.

The village of Cliddesdon survives, duckpond, ducks and all from just this happy chance. Cliddesdon Down House in the centre of the village is the old rectory; good red-brick late eighteenth-century, fronted by a gravel sweep and high hedges. The garden, not large, is on the south, west and north-west sides. It is full of interesting plants carefully chosen to succeed upon a soil of high alkalinity and provides useful lessons to those labouring under this cloud.

Against the corner of the house is *Phillyrea augustifolia*, a distinct evergreen with long netted leaves, and a couple of *Viburnum x burkwoodii*. A broad lawn surrounded by mature trees is dominated by a big beech and at the end the screen has been opened to give views of the succeeding meadow. To the left is a good snake-bark maple, *Acer pennsylvanica*, and behind the beech an interesting trio: *Staphylea colchica rosea* and *Magnolia kobus* growing fast, rivalled by a near vertical euonymus probably *E latifolia*, which colours well in autumn.

Back by the house a very broad paved terrace permits shrubs against the south west front to spill forward with only their back branches tied. Such luxuriance of effect is most satisfactory. Here are *Viburnum henryi*, *Carpenteria californica*, jasmines and roses with *Nerine bowdenii* at their base emphasising the subtle pink of nearby *Abelia x grandiflora*. Several different daphnes succeed admirably.

At the corner a well-clothed trellis separates this terrace from an even wider one to the north west. Under the house walls are two herbaceous beds concentrating upon soft yellow and white flowers and foliage. Ahead a dozen shallow steps (note plants of *Buddleia alternifolia* and *Cistus laurifolius* draped with *Clematis macropetala* on each side). The steps are centred upon a huge old apple tree which makes the focus for a densely planted early summer garden. Here are old-fashioned and species roses (including *R omeiensis pterocantha* with its wicked-looking scarlet thorns), philadelphuses, *Kolkwitzia amabilis* and *Magnolia x highdownensis.*

To the south is perhaps the only prunus 'Amanangowa' pergola in existence; certainly no-one would expect its vertical growths to take happily to tying down – but with care they do and the effect in late April is splendid.

The summer garden is separated from a swimming-pool garden to the north by a beech hedge and, beyond a south west facing wall holds roses and is fronted by an herbaceous border. An usual vine in the corner is *Ampelopsis brevipedunculata* with extraordinary turquoise fruit. Opposite on the house a big *Actinidia chinensis* also fruits well; this is the Chinese gooseberry, sometimes now called Kiwi fruit and the hermaphrodite forms, of which this must be one, have originated, not surprisingly, in New Zealand.

This garden continues to develop; woodland to the west is being opened up and a couple of *Acer griseum* are to be joined by others of this genus for autumn leaf colour effect. *Prunus subhirtella ascendens* and *P sargentii* have made fine young trees.

Cold Hayes

Steep Marsh, W of A325 road from Petersfield to Liss, 2 miles N of Steep.

Little Coldhayes refers to a modern house fitted into the east end of the main terrace of Cold Hayes, itself a rather splendid Victorian pile of 1881. The gardens of both can be considered together and consist of the south slope of the house terrace, with distant views to the downs, and supporting areas each side.

Fine trees on three sides protect the gardens and form an enclosure for the view. Against the house *Cytisus battandieri* flourishes – it doesn't really need a wall but its brittle growth appreciates protection while the downy leaves and spikes of yellow fruity-smelling flowers look well against fawn-grey stone. Here, too, also with grey leaves is *Teucrium fruticans*, a Mediterranean labiate too seldom seen.

The slope drops down in five levels. To the west a group of shrubs; a good *Magnolia kobus. M.soulangiana lennei* and *Acer griseum. Parottia persica*, always wider than high, here is as flat as the Lanarth form of

Viburnum tomentosum mariesii, and hence an interesting specimen.

It is from here, too, that the balancing trees and shrubs on the far side of the terrace should be examined, a splendid textural heap of grey, purple and shades of green. This is made up of *Cedrus atlantica glauca*, purple beech, sea buckthorn, cotinus and so on.

The main lower terrace is grandly designed around a large formal pool. Here are roses, herbaceous plants in quantity; the scale can be indicated by the fact that *Euphorbia charachias* ssp *wulfenii* seeds itself in the cracks in the paving and is not particularly in the way. Ground cover is sensibly used. All this is on wet heavy clay which permits, on one hand, astilbes in the borders, yet makes life difficult for many other things especially some of the roses.

By the small terrace of Little Coldhayes a flat rock garden or alpine meadow is remarkably successful in half-shade. The simpler plants — aubrieta, phlox, pulsatillas, sedums with small spring bulbs — give a mass of colour for a long period and are not particularly laboursome.

NOTEWORTHY SPECIMENS: *Magnolia grandiflora* on lowest terrace, purple beech, cut-leaved beech above kitchen garden.

Court Hall

At East Meon. Turn E from A32 at West Meon or S from A272 at Langrish. Fifteenth-century Ecclesiastical Hall also shown.

A series of architectural courtyard gardens on three sides of the impressive early fifteenth-century building with its later additions.

Having been demoted to a farm and the great hall itself divided into labourers' accommodation it fell to Morley Horder in the 1920's to restore the building and to contrive a suitable setting. In this he was entirely successful; yew hedges, broad flagged paths and wide borders give a feeling of age and peace. A recent swimming pool on an upper terrace (only rivalled by a tennis court as the most difficult feature to fit into a garden without ruining it) in no way offends. Below the pool, across another lawn is a new planting of old-fashioned roses and shrubs. An unclipped hedge of *Lonicera nitida* shows the potential of an under-rated plant; here its billowing curves contrast well with the severity of yew.

NOTEWORTHY SPECIMEN: *Hydrangea petiolaris* on south wall of the Hall.

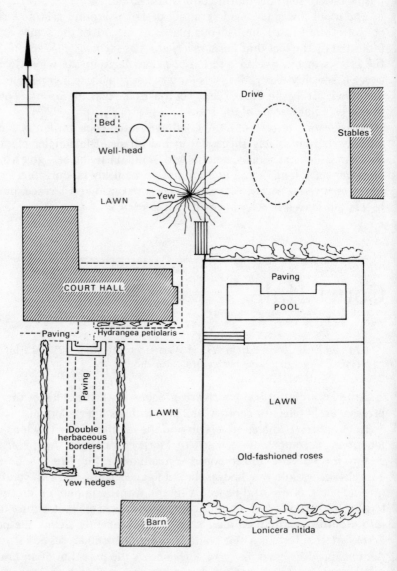

Cranbury Park

Otterbourne, 2 miles N of Eastleigh on *Old* A33 Southampton–Winchester road. Turn W at top of Otterbourne Hill.

Although a new dual trunk road skirts the eastern edge of the park and suburban sprawl from Southampton and its outliers encroaches from the south, Cranbury House sits, like a Queen on her throne, untouched in the middle of its broad domains.

Across the park an eighteenth-century Gothick folly composed of bits of the truly Gothic Netley Abbey on Southampton Water suggests an earlier period of landscape development and the splendid indigenous trees, oaks, beech and hornbeam confirm this; but the 20 acres or so of pleasure grounds around the house itself seem mainly contemporary with the 1830's alterations there by J.B. Papworth which are mentioned by Pevsner (*The Buildings of England: Hampshire*). The original design is by George Dance Jr.

A semicircular gravel sweep passes between a pair of unusually fine iron gates to the porte cochère at the south entrance front of what Pevsner with unusual fulsomeness, calls 'an amazing house, baffling outside and spacially daring and quite grandiose inside'.

The east front faces a circular pool with a high tiered fountain. Vases and Irish yews (which fruit well, brightening their darkness with innumerable points of scarlet light). Beyond is arboretum-like planting of now mature conifers and deciduous species with walks to the urn-topped ha-ha wall. From here views stretch out to south and east. Behind, ground falls away sharply to the north and a wide grass ride, enclosed by mazes of clipped rhododendron and laurel, follows the drop to a second circular pool. Glimpses through the trees show the wide chalkland countryside towards Winchester.

A further ride moving west (note *Magnolia virginiana* with exquisitely scented creamy-suède flowers and silvery undersides to its evergreen leaves) leads to a grotto protecting a gin-clear spring. The water is still used. A verse that William Wordsworth was moved to write here is carved at the back:

'Gentle Reader, view in Me
An Emblem of true Charity
Who, while my Bounty I bestow

Am neither heard nor seen to flow.
For ev'ry Drop of Water giv'n
Repaid by fresh Supplies from Heav'n.'

Cranbury's air seems to have caused the poet's usually impeccable muse to nod somewhat.

Above the grotto through the trees can be seen a charming garden-house with a little colonnade on each side. This is much in the mood of George Dance Jr, architect of the Cranbury itself. Near this gazebo house are two small enclosed gardens, the first with a central iron cage draped with climbers while the second is a charming period rose garden with box edges round the beds of old-fashioned varieties planted within.

The visitor has now reached the west side of the house beyond the stables (where family carriages are shown when the garden opens) and here is a hilltop plateau whose surrounding banks – thickly planted with trees and underplanted with flat-cut laurel – resemble (and perhaps they are) the outer defences of Romano-British earthworks. Within the circle a now roofless orangery is planted with peonies and delphiniums and near by is an old sundial having a particularly beautiful gnomon.

South west of the 'hill-fort' a meadow is crossed to a fine tree-girt lake, its circumlocutory walk lined with rhododendrons and recently planted azaleas. Beyond again is a walled kitchen garden.

NOTEWORTHY SPECIMENS: *Platanus x acerifolia* (London plane) by south front, *Sequoia sempervirens* (Big Tree of California) in arboretum, *Liriodendron tulipifera* (very old specimen north west of house), beeches and oaks.

The Dower House

Dogmersfield, 2 miles NE of Odiham. Turn N off A287 Farnham–Odiham road.

Cross the cattle grid by Dogmersfield church and a drive takes you over a swelling grass hill: beyond the brow is an imposing neo-Georgian building, built as a dower house for nearby Dogmersfield Park in 1930.

Immediately of interest at the south front is a small rose parterre enclosed by hedges – a yard high and as much wide – of *Pernettya mucronata*. This and the first sight of rhododendrons below the house indicates at once that the pH here is low. It is not the Bagshot Sands of only 10 miles further east but a decent sandy loam, remarkably moisture retentive.

This, in an old plantation area of 3 acres, has made possible a surprising woodland garden developed by the present owner over the last 15 years. Here under a high canopy of oaks, larch and birch all manner of ericaceous shrubs thrive. The *Grande* series rhododendrons are growing fast and cinnabarinums such as 'Golden Orfe' and 'Blandfordianum' do well. The high humidity causes an amount of green algae growth on the leaves; only the lack of grey lichen hanging from the branches of the trees indicates one is not in south Devon or Cornwall.

NOTEWORTHY SPECIMENS: *Magnolia grandiflora* (free standing), *Magnolia sieboldii*.

Drayton House

East Meon. Turn E from A32 at West Meon or S from A272.

The River Meon starts high up in the chalk downs near Petersfield by flowing from east to west. Drayton House lies not far from its source and well above its north bank, protected from north and east by natural woodland.

The garden, or more exactly gardens (for there are several cottage-like gardens) follow the contours of their hillside linked by brick paths and steps; the old retaining walls make suitable homes for self-sown buddleias and valerian (the white is an especially good plant). Artifice has been used to copy nature by inserting regal pelargoniums into the holes of a kitchen garden wall.

Specialities are chalk-suitable old-fashioned roses, peonies, iris, soft grey and purple foliage plants. Shade is provided by gnarled old apples and cherries.

From the colonnaded south front of the early nineteenth-century house a fine view is enjoyed of Downs across the croquet lawn.

NOTEWORTHY SPECIMENS: Fine walnuts.

Empshott Wood

1½ miles S of Selborne. Turn S off B3006 Liss—Selborne road, or approach eastwards from East Tisted on A32.

Neither the house nor the garden have existed in this hitherto open field for more than a dozen years. But in that time a feeling of maturity has settled upon the site which will give comfort to those who feel their garden bareness will never be clothed, and, who, too, manage their garden themselves.

At the top of a steep drive the elegant white clapboard house with a Kentish (or even Williamsburg) feel stands high on its terrace. Between rose-hung clunch retaining walls a dozen steps mount to the front door. Only from the short path here do other parts of the garden come into view. Directly under the house front are grey foliage plants and white flowers; the rather tender *Senecio leucostachys* (a brittle beauty, which as at West Tytherley, is clearly happier scrambling through something else), curry plant, rosemary, and *Anthemis cupaniana*. This white and grey daisy occurs frequently at Empshott Wood and is a valuable cover in full sun. An enormous mound of *Senecio greyii* softens a house corner.

From here the bank, which is the west side of the garden (but east facing with views way into Sussex) is seen; informal plantings of old-fashioned and other shrub roses in carefully graduated colour sequences. Behind, a shrub border with emphasis on foliage where *Cytisus battandieri* gives its pineapple scented bonus of yellow flowers. More shrub roses border a croquet lawn.

NOTEWORTHY SPECIMENS: A eucalyptus species, (probably *E.gunnii*) by garage, 10 years old and *huge*. A beautiful tree.

Durmast House

Burley, off A35 Lyndhurst—Bournemouth road. Turn W at Wilverley Post.

This is another Jekyll garden in Burley with a somewhat complicated plan now upset by the splendid growth, in the intervening three-quarters of a century, of enormous trees.

As with so many New Forest gardens the house is placed near the road thus opening its terrace doors onto garden, woodland and view. There are three main areas, virtually separate from each other: a shady lawn with fine specimen trees, particularly deodar and Monterey pine; then a central area in front of the terrace − from which it is divided by topiary yews − is a rose garden whose large beds are sub-divided by lavender hedges. Here one bed has been completely lost under the shade of one of the biggest cut-leaved beeches in the country. Behind it a brick wall and inevitable Jekyllesque pergola supports venerable wisteria and *W.sinensis multijuga*. The palest lavender racemes of the latter reach 2 ft in length, and, as contrast, the wall is also covered with polypody fern.

Finally there is a rock garden, a pool and groups of herbaceous plants in the quantity and quality that Miss Jekyll would have approved. NOTEWORTHY SPECIMENS: *Eagus sylvatica heterophylla, Cedrus deodara, Pinus radiata, Choisya ternata.*

Exbury

15 miles SW of Southampton. Take the B3053 from the A35 then the B3054 at Dibden Purlieu.

Although records have been lost it would appear that the big house of Exbury is contemporary with the mature cedars that cluster near it. This would put an early nineteenth-century date to it; but its present aspects, with views from the colonnaded south front across the ha-ha to the Solent and Isle of Wight beyond, are the product of its becoming a Rothschild estate in 1919. In 2 years, after extensive alterations, the house was ready for occupation and work on the garden began.

As with all gardens this has, of course, never stopped and the near 200 acres are the product of a half-century of development and exten-sion. On its very acid soil, shaded by high-canopy oak and Scots pine woodland it is not surprising that rhododendrons have pride of place, nor in this climatically favourable spot with sea on two sides, that Exbury has the most complete collection of rhododendron species in the

British Isles. These have been used as stock material for the vast number of fine hybrids bred here since the 1920's and this work is still going on as new species are brought in. For example Exbury has been responsible for the introduction of the Japanese *R.yakusimanum* which has brought new life into rhododendrons for small gardens.

Exbury is of such a size and has such confusing complexity of paths to follow that it is a mistake to try and 'do' it in one visit. Indeed, although a rhododendron garden par excellence the range of plants and interest is such that no one period displays all its pleasure and possibilities. The map shows only the main areas; smaller delights are to be discovered personally.

On leaving the car park the edge of Home Park is crossed. This 'front lawn' as it might be termed were it not acres in extent, is dotted with commemorative trees planted by illustrious visitors. As at Broadlands (cf.) their plaques give valuable information as to speed of growth and possibly finger-greenness of the notability concerned; particularly fine is a 25 ft high *Picea breweriana* planted in 1930 by the Countess of Harewood.

Crossing the entrance court of Exbury House with its huge *Magnolia delavayi* – this seems very much a Hampshire plant; it can look so sad and tatty when not suited – the garden proper is entered through the Holly Tunnel, its dark enclosure suddenly opening up into the Long Glade. Here under cedars and great oaks some of the earlier plantings have reached fine maturity.

It is probably best at this point not to follow the glade to its end but to branch south west and downhill towards the ponds. The main walk and its branches are lined with rhododendrons of all kinds, large and small, species and hybrid. Magnolias add height with fine specimens of *M campbellii* (to be seen most years flowering in early March), *M salicifolia* with lemon-scented bark and others. An unusual conifer here is the Chilean *Podocarpus salignus* with its piles of soft-green willow-like leaves. More conventionally here too are good specimens of sitka spruce and swamp cypress. Great planes have fallen yet not died to provide a theatre of living sculpture or adventure playground, depending upon one's age and inclinations.

A lawn slopes down to High Pond bordered with candelabra primulas and overhung with wisteria. This is an area particularly devoted to the deciduous azaleas which Exbury has made famous and which bear its name. North of the pond a shallow dell contains a wide selection of these: it is known as theWinniatt Bowl in honour of the well-known head gardener who cared for the gardens for many years.

Other good plants abound: Japanese maples, cercidiphyllum with

4   Jenkyn Place. The Sundial Garden with a view south through the apple arch underplanted with crinums

5   Topiary at the northwest corner of Mottisfont Abbey

flame-coloured autumn tints and *Salix fargesii* where the stream enters the pond. This is the most unlikely willow – thick 6 in. long leaves and scarlet buds.

Beyond Low Pond with its island the most exciting plantings are of the Exbury-raised big-leaved hybrid of *Rhododendron* 'Fortune'. These are not things for small gardens, such plants have to be visited, admired and left alone (rather like Nelson's column). 'Fortune' was bred from Exbury's own mother plant of *Rhododendron falconeri* with pollen from the Trewithen form of *R.sinogrande*. The offspring first flowered in 1938 and was immediately awarded an F.C.C. by the Royal Horticultural Society. The huge trusses of 25 or so flowers are rich yellow and each flower has a crimson patch in the throat. A mouthwatering plant indeed.

A path to the east now leads back to High Pond through camellias where *C.japonica* 'Lady Clare', low in habit with lustrous leaves makes a valuable foliage plant even out of flower. Further camellias, including old plants of *C.reticulata* 'Captain Rawes' and the exquisite *C.j.* 'magno-liaeflora' can be found in Home Wood. Here, too, are thickets of hamamelis which light up the darkest days of winter.

The path to the view point leads north from High Pond. Here it is possible to relax without further claims upon the eye than are made by broad distant views across the daffodil meadow (different forms in flower from February until the show ends with pheasant-eye narcissus in June) to the Beaulieu River and the New Forest beyond. When rested one may return via Long Glade – certainly a half-day visit has already been accomplished – or continue into Witcher's Wood (noting on the way *Wistaria sinensis multijuga* with yard-long racemes of flowers on the tennis-court pergola).

Lovers Lane is crossed at right angles, leading from the house to Gilbury Pond. It and its side-shoots are densely planted with many plants of interest, which only frequent visits over a period of time can encompass. But *the* time to go, without doubt, is, in normal years, late May, for the beauty of Lady Chamberlain's Walk. Lady Chamberlain is a *Rhododendron cinnabarinum* hybrid – first raised at Exbury and awarded an F.C.C. in 1931. These are thus amongst the finest specimens any-where – and this long curving path is lined with them. Growth is tall and thin, leaves are small and blue-green, often attractively waved and the flowers are waxy, drooping, and like narrow bells. They appear in all soft shades from mandarin red, through clear orange to salmon-pink and yellow. The sight is, as they say, one for sore eyes.

Lady Chamberlain's Walk joins the main drive just below the classical bridge that crosses, not a river, but a public road. It is marked by high

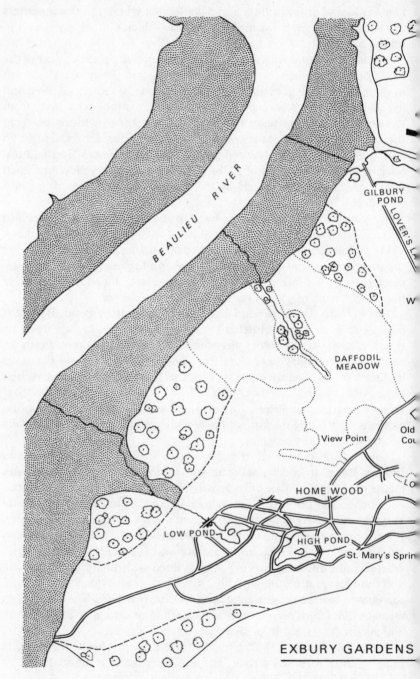

EXBURY GARDENS

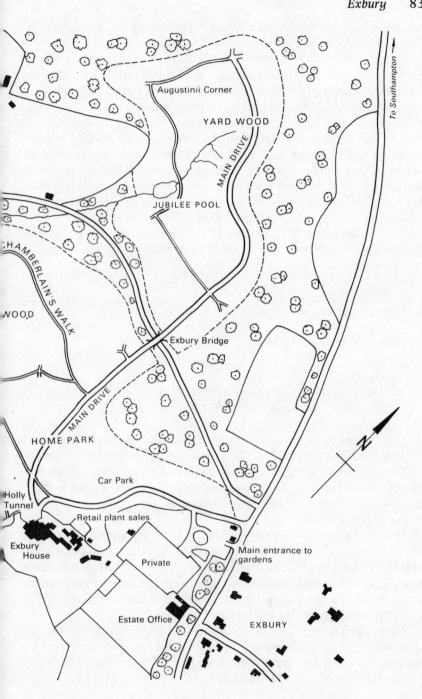

columnar Dawyck beeches and Italian cypresses. As the map shows, the drive continues for some long way and a circuit can be made to enjoy the extensive plantings of near-blue *R.augustinii*, its hybrids and forms (in May) in the northernmost corner of the grounds. Fortunately the same lovely plant can be seen nearer at hand; a particularly felicitous grouping with the blue-leaved *Eucalyptus urnigera* can be found in Witcher's Wood.

New development and new planting continues and where it does the daunting soil of stones and sand can be seen no longer covered by carpets of moss or shrub growth. Even gardeners with the smallest patch can learn from techniques used here; lots of humus incorporated and a thick layer of leaf-mould kept in place by a circlet of wire netting (also anti-rabbit) round every young plant. No doubt it is this sort of individual care, over 50 years or so, that helps to make a garden famous.
NOTEWORTHY SPECIMENS: Too many to mention.

Fairfield House

N end of Hambledon village on the B2150. 10 miles NW of Portsmouth, 9 miles SW of Petersfield. Approached from the A3 or A32.

At the bottom of the chalky, flint-filled hill that makes the wine from Hambledon Vineyard (see Little Down) so distinctive, Fairfield House has rather more depth of soil and the desirable shade that only mature trees can provide. Here then is a background for the interesting garden which the relatively recent owners are developing fast around a charming white Regency house.

The circular drive, under fine Cedars of Lebanon, surrounds an area filled with spring bulbs. To the left the main front of the house with its pair of bay windows looks across lawn to a screen of mainly indigenous trees. Under the walls are abelias and a big *Hebe cupressoides* entirely living up to its specific epithet to resemble a dwarf conifer, which suddenly and improbably bursts into flower.

A big curving border, extravagantly planted, takes the eye from a less than pretty Victorian accretion to the house. Here *Rosa turkestanica* is noteworthy as is, near by, a huge lime tree. This, having been stooled in youth has now a thicket of trunks.

The east-facing slope to the west, once walled kitchen garden, is now being developed ornamentally with unusual trees and shrubs. The remarkable *Sorbus sargentiana*, introduced from West China by Wilson in 1904 is doing well with its great heads of scarlet fruits and crimson 'sticky-buds'.

At the bottom of the slope an oval swimming pool is associated with a well-clothed (note *Solanum jasminoides album*) pergola and a border of white flowers and grey foliage. Looking up to the left in deep shade a group of big-leaved plants, including *Viburnum rhytidophyllum*, makes a good eye-catcher.

Through a gate in the northern kitchen garden wall an area known as Mesopotamia (though the two rivers are not noticeable!) leads back down the slope; plants tumbling against a wall include the 'lemon peel' *Clematis tangutica* and the autumn flowered *C.x jouiniana*.

A more formal area north of the house is now reached which concentrates on roses in soft yellows and pinks. An east border is devoted to impressive-leaved herbaceous plants including *Geranium psilostemon* (outstanding with magenta, black-eyed flowers) *Crambe cordifolia* and euphorbias. On the wall is the lovely pink *Robinia kelseyi*, and *Clematis armandii*. Also remarkable in an area noted for its vines is the Vine house here.

Fir Hill

4½ miles N of Droxford, midway between Alton and Portsmouth. At N end of village on the A32.

Any front garden for Fir Hill, a good 1767 pale red-brick house off the main street of Droxford is made both impossible and unnecessary by a vast Atlas cedar which dominates all.

North of the house the main garden is reached by 9 curved steps through a pretty herringboned brick courtyard. Thymes grow on the flat and other herbs tumble over the retaining walls; rue seeds itself about.

Behind the house a broad south east lawn slopes to the River Meon. A sweeping shrub border faces south west and the view is half hidden by fine young liriodendron – the tulip tree of south east U.S.A. – which flowers in June. To the right the kitchen garden is enclosed by high thuja hedges. This gives a stronger texture than the now almost ubiquitous Leyland cypress.

Fir Hill frequently shares its open day with other gardens in this charming village. All are of interest and show different ways of dealing with similar problems of climate and soil: the former is equable, the latter thin and stony above chalk.

Froyle Mill

Froyle, 4 miles NE of Alton, 1 mile S of Bentley on S side of A31 Alton–Farnham road.

A steep lane drops down from the busy A31 to the peace of theWey valley. Froyle Mill and its Mill house make, as watermills so often do, a charming picture of solid vernacular architecture above the shimmer of moving water. Although the garden as now seen is only 7 years old the 1760's buildings give an air of great maturity.

East of the house (its entrance front) is a small 'cottage garden' – in its sophisticated garden-design sense. Fronting its fence against the lane is a narrow border of low tumbling grey and purple-leaved shrubs, sages, rue, *Senecio greyi*, lavender and so on to set the scene. Behind are lilies, and other simple herbaceous plants to give interest over a long season, honey-suckles and old-fashioned roses. The crimson 'Charles de Mills' is particularly fine. More roses are planted on the steep bank above; hybrid musks, rugosas, even hybrid teas are in rough grass which is cut every three weeks in summer and the hay laid around the shrubs as a moisture-retaining and anti-weed mulch.

A path winds along this bank above the house, eventually leading down to the main garden on its other side. It is better, however, to see this first from a lower level. Entrance is by the south end of the mill. Through a narrow gate the view suddenly opens up – mill pool, weir and broad expanse of water meadows across and upstream. To the right in the space – not large – between buildings and bank a most unusual conception has been built up. The owners maintain that Japanese gardens have, in essence, been taken as exemplars, although the end effect clearly cannot be truly oriental. Certainly here is the scaled down landscape, careful placing of rock, water and plant material. Exuberance and diversity of the latter, however felicitous their combinations (and these are many) make the garden blessedly occidental. The choice of plants is in no way bound by tradition. It suffices that all are good and do what is required of them.

Marsh plants, not surprisingly, do well. Hardy arums, *Trollius europaeus*, primulas, *Gentiana asclepiadea*, and the tiny rare native *Anagallis tenella*, species needing less moisture, are catered for by the hills and rocky areas; here many unusual alpines succeed, some of which have been collected from their Himalayan homes. Dwarf bulbs give interest at all times of the year and golden pearlwort (which now carries a name vastly bigger than itself: *Minuartia verna caespitosa aurea*) has been effectively used to equate with the moss of Japanese gardens. Against the house are several good plants wisely concentrating on scent, beginning the year with wintersweet and *Azara microphylla*. A pergola carries further climbers, below which is a bank of finely chosen foliage plants – ericas, hebes, cistus, *Chamaecyparis pisifera filifera aurea* (worth its monstrous name) with phormium and the tall grass *Stipa gigantea* adding exclamation marks.

Further good plants and interesting combinations move up the bank. Throughout, the thought that has gone into design and the care into cultivation and maintenance is very apparent.

Furzey

Minstead. Open throughout the year 10–7 (dusk in winter). 3 miles NW of Lyndhurst. Turn S of A31 Cadnam–Ringwood road.

The garden at Furzey has been justly famous for 50 years both amongst knowledgeable plantsmen and those who, more simply but with no less validity, recognise quality when they see it. The long, low, thatched house was built on open Forest pasture land in 1922 for the three Dalrymple brothers, one of whom in his nearby nursery at Bartley produced so many good plants which still bear that name. The 8 acres of south-facing slope were laid out informally with winding paths between banks and beds of trees and shrubs. Only in the early years was herbaceous material greatly used; now there is little.

In the late 1950's and 60's, with the death of the original owners Furzey fell into decline; this is now halted and new owners, continuing the tradition of their predecessors by allowing visitors throughout the year, are beginning with a staff of two to repair the ravages of neglect. In such a specialist garden this is not easy. Entrance is now by the side of the old staff cottage to the east of the main house from which, after an area of open grass, the ground falls away. Already plants can be seen to emerge from the mass of material which are either quite unfamiliar or if they do ring a bell in the horticultural memory it immediately occurs to the mind that they have no right to be *that big*. Eucryphias, snowy heaps in late summer, are good examples; *E.cordifolia* and the deciduous *E.glutinosa* are fine plants while the famous hybrid between them *E. x nymansensis* is over 40 ft high – a tower of dark green when not in flower. The magpies which nest in it here obviously have very good taste.

From the top lawn it is probably best to drift down to the left; at any time of the year there will be interest – often on a dramatic scale. A huge (the epithet is almost inevitable at Furzey) *Corylopsis platypetala* is good in February with primrose yellow 'catkins'; further down and in other parts of the garden a rather thin evergreen tree appears frequently, suckering about. In late May and early June these Chilean fire-trees (embothrium) will be astonishing pillars of vermilion. I know of no garden where they flourish so.

Although there are banks of azaleas, this is generally not a rhododendron garden, being perhaps too hot for most of the best woodland species. So one is even more surprised down here to find, in full sun, a great domed big-leaved rhododendron – probably *R.macabeanum*. It bounds a small lawn across which *Primula prolifera* and *Iris kaemferi* follow a moist ditch, their yellow and purple combining very effectively.

Further to the south east a wide pool has been recently made to extend Furzey's scope. Returning back towards the house the visitor may either follow a path against the lower, southern boundary or zig-zag up and down the slope to see what each path brings. He should, of course, do both. In spring, tree heaths and magnolias are predominant and the seasons progress through azaleas, dogwoods, lantern-trees (crinodendrons, 12 ft high), eucryphias and autumn colour of nyssa, parrotia and enkianthus. Bulbs below add their seasonal bit in wide swathes from rare exotics to indigenous bluebells under the huge forest oaks which the new garden used as focal points.

The area that is now approached below the house is really a heather garden on a vast scale; callunas, *Daboecia cantabrica*, pernettyas and ericas in vast variety give 12 month interest. In summer the wands of 'angels' fishing-rods' (*Dierama pulcherrima*) which seeds itself around, hang out in all directions, softly pink and purple.

Ground now falls away south westward ending in a copse of high Scots pine; framed against them is a 40 ft high *Betula utilis*.

The routes back to the cottage and entrance are several; each and every one will offer plants of interest and beauty, many of them unlikely to have been seen elsewhere. Only identification is a difficulty. Furzey was, of course, one of the gardens to which new collected material from the Orient and especially Australasia came. Hence these plants are often of historical value. An inevitable difficulty for the present owners and their staff is the well-being and maintenance of such stuff while continuing to replant that which is past its best. Unlike other works of art a garden, however perfect, cannot remain at that peak of perfection; it either moves forward or inevitably moves back.

NOTEWORTHY SPECIMENS: Too many to list.

Fyning Manor

5 miles E of Petersfield on the A272, ¼ mile E of Rogate village.

A flinty track west of Rogate, so strictly West Sussex and not Hampshire at all, turns in front of the south front of Fyning Manor. Across the drive wide mixed borders have a June predominance of roses – shrub and old-fashioned – and tree lupins. These combine to give a particularly heady fragrance. To the east is a huge *Magnolia soulangiana* (another is on the house; prospective planters should note how big they may become).

On this side of the house a bank rises, solidly planted with lavenders, hypericums and, for winter effect, heathers. The front door is approached by a small but charming flagged raised court. This could be a town garden in miniature and is full of interesting plants: *Erigeron mucronatus. Raphiolepis umbellata* – an evergreen rosaceous shrub, *Rosa banksiae* on the house. Note, as you pass to the lawn garden a huge clump of the regal fern, *Osmunda regalis*. The tall old apple trees in this garden are draped with mistletoe. A mixed border of roses, herbaceous plants and shrubs leads to a seat, which is flanked by a fine pair of Mediterranean cypresses. This true *Cupressus sempervireus stricta* is

seldom seen in Britain but clearly can make a good specimen.
NOTEWORTHY SPECIMENS: *Camellia sasanqua,* Scots pine, *Clematis armandii*
on garage, *Mespilus germanica* (medlar).

Greatham Mill

Liss, 5 miles N of Petersfield. From A325 Petersfield–Farnham road turn
W at Greatham. After 600 yards turn left into 'No Through Road'.

Here is a garden of little more than an acre, yet because of its planning
and wealth of exciting plants the appearance is given of much more.

A narrow lane leads down to the long low south front of the 1690's
mill. The forecourt is uneven with worn flags and setts in crevices of
which flowers *Erigeron mucronatus,* that little South African daisy
which establishes itself (if one is lucky) in walls and paving. Against the
house *Convolvulus cneorum,* the shrubby bindweed from South Italy,
scrambles 6 ft high. Standard fuchsias stand out in groups for the
summer.

Beyond a low wall a lawn contains broad island beds and plantings
in the now dry bed of the mill-race; shrubs, primulas, musks with effective swathes of ground cover. Throughout the seasons there are both
individual plants of interest and felicitous groupings.

Between two barns (with a very large wintersweet against one) a
footbridge over the stream leads to the small nursery where plants
admired at Greatham Mill can be purchased, and to the right a gate to
the other two-thirds of the garden. Immediately arresting is a small flat
rock bed, all over thymes, helianthemums backed by a great heap of
foliage shrubs. These in particular are a feature of Greatham Mill.
Cornus stolonifera elegantissima, cut-leaved elder, *Heracleum mantegazzianum* (the giant hogweed) and gunnera. There is a heap of golden
foliage; *Robinia* 'Frisia', variegated hostas and thymes, golden elder and
Lonicera nitida. Near by, gold is the flower colour in a combination
which combines it with grey and purple. Even on the rock garden
foliage plants can be found, the rare black-leaved ophiopogon, *Phormium*
'Baby Bronze' and so on.

Much of this upper garden is in a big bend of the stream and towards
the top are new plantings of trees and unusual shrubs. Return by the

dell and a flat lawn (once a tennis court, which accounts for the clinker in some of the surrounding beds; the plants do not seem to mind). The retaining wall border offers many plants of interest – the tall grass, *Stipa gigantea*, eryngiums, a double form of our native sea campion and ground-hugging *Ceanothus procumbens*.

Greatham Mill offers plant interest at all seasons of the year and is open frequently to make such visits possible.

NOTEWORTHY SPECIMEN: Wisteria on the house.

Harcombe House

Leave A31 Alton–Winchester road at The Anchor, Ropley. Follow road to West Tisted for ½ mile. Turn up the first narrow lane on right to Harcombe.

At first sight the red-brick Dutch gables of Harcombe House give a seventeenth-century air but closer views confirm a *c.*1900 date. The 6 acres or so of garden mainly to the west and south of the house are immaculate. Broad lawns, carefully grouped trees – in surprisingly large and hence effective numbers, 9 *Prunus subhirtella autumnalis* for example.

Such groups are the product of the owners' plantings over the last 20 years or so, others are the result of gradual extension of the garden into the surrounding woodland. This, clearly, had been 'plantation' material so that the clearing and selection of specimens to be retained has left a host of trees with tall straight trunks and a high canopy. Around these are larch, ash and oak. Therefore good conditions are provided for shrub borders and beds planted on the grandest scale; many plants have reached maturity and combine to make splendid effects of texture and form.

Except in one smallish area which has some calcifuge species it has sensibly been decided not to fight the shallow flinty soil over chalk. Concentration upon genera which are lime tolerant such as viburnum and cotoneaster shows what remarkable diversity these garden-worthy groups possess. Blueness in hydrangeas is contrived not by aluminium sulphate but naturally, with *H.villosa* here over 12 ft high.

Conifers do particularly well, and around a pool with its pumped cascade a combination of *Juniperus sabina tamariscifolia* and others will be noted. Near the pool alongside the drive a most satisfactory association of plants has been created. A bed some 30 ft by 10 contains, inter alia, swathes of *Erica herbacea* whose colour is repeated by 6 ft bushes of *Berberis thunbergii atropurpurea* behind which is *Genista aetnensis*. By the time this is out in midsummer the erica is over and the berberis changes to a role of contrast. On a much smaller scale a combination of interesting shrubs, sweeping down to the formal pool behind the house is excellent. It is such miniatures which bring a big garden a personal feeling, and they are worth searching out by every visitor intent on improving his own patch.

Harcombe House also boasts a useful range of glass, a fine kitchen garden and plant interest throughout the year. A staff of three maintain it impeccably.

NOTEWORTHY SPECIMENS: Group of young 30 ft deodars, variegated acers.

Heather Lodge

Bransgore, 4 miles N of Christchurch. Turn off the A35 N at Hinton Admiral, then NE in Bransgore village on Burley road.

In a relatively small area, perhaps a half acre of cultivated ground and about the same of woodland, there are to be found here a wider range of interesting species than can usually be seen in much larger gardens. And not just good plants grown by a collector, but good plants well arranged to make a cohesive and most satisfying whole.

A small area north of the house contains a few rhododendrons, notably forms of *R.cinnabarinum*, whose blue leaves continue to be attractive after the flowers are gone. On the house the marbled *Vitis henryana* enjoys the shade; opposite on the garage is by far the best of the potato vines, *Solanum jasminoides album*.

Through a gate is the main garden, west and south of the house, sweeping beds edged with logs contain carefully graduated and juxta-posed species. Interesting calcifuge trees, such as *Styrax japonica*, give colour when the rhododendrons (almost all are forms with good leaves) are over. Below are ferns, *Gentiana asclepiadea* and *G.sino-ornata* while maianthemum and *Gaultheria procumbens* act as even lower ground cover. Ornamental grasses add delicate height.

To the south, garden merges into woodland with birch, oak and old *Rhododendron ponticum* thicket. Common though these are the effect in flower is spectacular while below, in dense shade, the fallen blossoms resemble improbably huge colonies of *Lathraea clandestina* — that odd parasite of willows which flowers in February.

West of the main lawn, past a 'ponticum' bowed down with *Akebia quinata*, is hidden a small serpentine pool and nearby peat-block wall. This is backed with an unusual hedge firstly of tree heather, *Erica arborea alpina*, then of *Cryptomeria japonica elegans*. As it emerges into the open it gives way to an old-fashioned rose to frame a border of non-calcifuge things — roses and herbaceous plants.

Behind the hedge the kitchen garden contains a fruit cage with, in addition to the conventional soft fruits, some North American blue-berries, so often recommended, so seldom seen.

Heather Lodge wastes no inch of space, the only sight of soil is where, in June for instance, a patch of *Cyclamen hederifolium* has gone to rest for a month or two. Even then the coiled-spring stems of the seed capsules give interest.

Highclere Castle

On W side of A34 Newbury–Winchester road, midway between Newbury and Whitchurch, 7 miles from each.

Driving off the busy A34 into the Carnarvon estate of Highclere Castle one moves into another, earlier and altogether more spacious world. A triumphal arch, no longer used as entry, has given suitable hints of this, but the belt plantings are so thick and the road itself so tortuous as to deserve full attention and preclude importunate peeping, that the surprise is complete.

Broad parkland undulates in all directions; no building, from here, not even the once obligatory ruined folly, interrupts the Elysian scene. Every tree, exotic and indigenous alike, appears at a peak of maturity; cattle group themselves aesthetically. At a bigger than usual group of cedars the drive turns south and suddenly, through the branches, a vision of pinnacles, machicolations and towers topped with a lazily flapping flag appears. This is no mediaeval castle, haunt of dark doings of dastardly dukes but a Walter Scott scene where all knights are chivalrous and every wimpled lady pure and probably beautiful into the bargain.

A clearly eighteenth-century lodge against the north front ha-ha indicates, surprisingly perhaps, that the great Barry house (Sir Charles was of course also architect of the present Houses of Parliament) replaces an earlier building and, moving further into the pleasure grounds a pillared classical temple to the east confirms the suspicion that all was suitably (and almost inevitably) landscaped by Lancelot ('Capability') Brown in the 1770's. This accounts particularly for the vast cedars of great age that grow in extraordinary profusion. Highclere is the ideal place to sort out one's cedar – identification ability. The rules are not irrevocable though generally quite safe; the Mount Atlas cedars in both the green and glaucous forms have upward growing branch tips – like pinions of a soaring buzzard; the North Indian deodar – classic tree of Victorian vicarage lawns – is a narrower tree, often with a single trunk, and pendulous branchlets. *Cedrus libani* has, in maturity, a flat top and near-horizontal branches. All three species are here in text-book perfection.

From the south front, 11 bays plus the corner towers wide with 'Ung je serviray' (one will I serve) carved in golden stone on every ground floor lintel, a vast lawn drops away to the densely treed valley. Beyond, the steep chalk downs are equally afforested. Further trees canalise the vista and are underplanted by quantities of naturalised daffodils; new forms are still being planted annually.

To the left an arched wall following the slope indicates a garden area. The scale of castle and surrounding trees makes this formal garden, though not small, seem almost irrelevant to the general scene, hence, no doubt, its seclusion and main use for providing quantities of cut flowers and, from the greenhouses, pot plants for the house.

The walled garden, with trained stone fruit (plums, peaches, nectarines) and seasonal plants, is divided into two by the great swelling bastions of a yew hedge. Above are four yew arches and a pair of pawns over 20 ft high. A door in the bottom wall leads to an area of winding grass paths and wide mixed borders planted particularly for spring and midsummer effect. Here are good cherries and magnolias and lesser things.

Further east a magnificent lime avenue, closely planted, leads south to Beacon Hill, on whose Romano-British fortified top the 5th Lord Carnarvon (especially remembered for his patronage of the Tutenk-hamun excavations and with Howard Carter a victim, some say, of the Pharaohs' curse, is buried). Turning left to the north end of the avenue it is possible to approach the temple from behind and to view the romantic castle through its reasonable columns; a nice juxtaposition of ideals. This is emphasised further when, on leaving the demesne by the lodge a distant rotunda is glimpsed to the north east indicating the extent of the early landscaping. Half Hampshire seems to be involved.

The soil is loam and clay-with-flints in varying depths over chalk; groups of quite large hardy hybrid rhododendrons appear to be in prepared soil.

NOTEWORTHY SPECIMENS: Too many to list.

Highcroft

Burley, off A35 Lyndhurst–Bournemouth road. Turn W at Wilverley Cross. Highcroft is opposite village cricket ground.

One of two adjacent Jekyll gardens (the other being Littlehay q.v.). Here the house, again by Clough, 1902, faces a typical New Forest woodland track and hence the garden is all to the south, itself carved from the forest whose great oaks make a backdrop.

Little more than the Jekyll outline remains; parallel thuya hedges enclose the main vista from the house which had been made to centre on a great ash tree. This, unfortunately, has died (an indication of the mutability of gardens). Behind, an apse of cleared forest contains an early planting of deciduous azaleas whose delicate colouring and open habit put to shame many modern hybrids.

The lawn contains a pair of pergolas, one with a fine wisteria and a small herbaceous garden. The four parallel borders, often a feature (now impossibly labour-intensive) of Jekyll design, have disappeared.

On a raised bed by the terrace the lovely grey foliage and yellow flowers of the perennial nasturtium *Tropaeolum polyphyllum*, is seen tumbling over the wall.

Hill House

From Alresford High Street take the B3046 towards Basingstoke. At Old Alresford church turn right.

Hill House stands close behind the lofty flint wall which screens its two acre garden from the road. The inner side of this wall carries a fine range of roses – mainly climbing sports of hybrid tea origin – and, to extend the season of flower, several clematis, a combination which extends to the main garden front of the house itself.

This front looks south and west across wide lawns to a screen of tall, mainly indigenous, trees. Further to the west the lawns continue and enclose a small formal garden.

The garden's north boundary on this side backs a broad herbaceous border generously planted for summer-long effect. Reached from the gravel sweep behind the house the productive kitchen garden is also worth a visit.

Hillier Arboretum

Open Monday–Friday 9–4.30. In Jermyns Lane, Ampfield, 2½ miles NE of Romsey off A31 Winchester–Romsey road.

The remarkable gardens and arboretum around Jermyns House fulfil three particular roles. Firstly they are the private collections of a well-known plantsman which are continually being added to – already perhaps 15,000 different plants have been accumulated. Secondly these make a reservoir of material which the Hillier nurseries can use for propagation. And thirdly this is a vast show-case that visitors can use to compare species, to choose for their own gardens or merely admire on the spot.

Most aspects of decorative gardening can be seen but clearly the emphasis is upon trees and shrubs for which Hillier's Nurseries are justly famed.

Visitors leave their cars in the nursery yard and walk round to the east front of the pretty 1850's house. From here ground slopes up gently and wide scree beds fill the foreground whilst the eye travels beyond to beds of massed shrubs and a backdrop of trees whose silhouettes – frequently unrecognized – encourage one to explore further and further.

The screes contain an extensive collection of so-called dwarf conifers, but frequently their size after 20 years belies the name. All plants grow through a 2 in. layer of pea gravel; this sets them off well,

1. Abbotsbury: Thick woodland on the seaward side gives protection to delicate exotics

Abbotsbury: Cinnamon-red
nks of *Myrtus apiculata* from
le

3. *left* Athelhampton

4. *below* The great south front of Forde
Abbey from the canal

5. *Pieris japonica* in woodland at Forde Abbey

6. The Japanese Garden at Compton Acres

7. North front of Cranbourne Manor. The White Garden is within the gate at the end of the elm avenue

8. Bramdean House: looking south from the kitchen garden gate

9. Jenkyn Place; old bush apples underplanted with crinums

10. Formality at Court House, East Meon: the south front from the herbaceous garden

11. *Wisteria sinensis macrobotrys* at Durmast House, Burley

12. Rhododendron 'Fortune' at Exbury: one of the famous hybrids raised here

13. Acers and rhododrons at Exbury

14. The double herbaceous borders edged with catmint at Kings Chantry

15 & 16. Harcombe House: *left*, the lower pool edged with contrasting shrubs; *below*, the formal pool behind the house

17 & 18. Hinton Ampner House:
left, view to the west looking across
the ha-ha; *below*, to the east of the
house where the ground falls away
in a series of steps

19 & 20. Jenkyn Place: *above*, the circular herb garden seen through its hedge of Penzance briars; *below*, the double herbaceous borders and, on the left, the great cedar by the house

21 & 22. Longstock Water Gardens: *left*, water lilies and marginal plants; *below*, huge leaves of gunnera and lysichitum

23 & 24. Old Rectory, West Tytherley: *right*, a cottagey border of roses and herbaceous plants; *below*, paeonies, irises and phlox in the kitchen garden

25. *left, Convolvulus cneorum* at Greatham Mill

26. *below, Phormium tenax* and rhododendrons at Pylewell Park

27. *right, above* A lily pool at Tunworth Old Rectory. Yuccas at the corners emphasize its formality

28. *right, below* Spinners, Boldre: rhododendrons and other shrubs seen looking west from above the house

29. New plantings of azaleas and primulas at The Wylds, Liss

makes access easy and, of course helps with maintenance. This last factor in all the areas is of prime importance; the 120 acres is serviced by only 5 men. Seasonal colour on the screes is provided by broad swathes of small bulbs and other alpines. In summer quantities of the lovely wand-flower, *Dierama pulcherrima* make a fine effect.

Behind a backing beech hedge to the north lies the 'tender garden' where many doubtfully hardy shrubs are tried out. This is for the incorrigible plantsman who will never learn to let well alone. More reasoned visitors will walk up the lawns beyond the screes and gradually meander back through the plantings on the southern boundary. Note should be made of two particularly exquisite Australasian gums; *Eucalyptus nitens*, a 50 ft infant prodigy, straight as a die and only 8 years old; and a perfect specimen, typically leaning, of *E.niphophila*, the snow gum. This route brings one down through mature camellias, a great belt of which continues to follow, crossing the front drive to the house, the Jermyns Lane boundary. Here are extensive groups of *C.japonica* forms and hybrids, the great *C. x williamsii* clan, (*C. x w.* 'Donation' is always lauded in the books; here even flowerless bushes indicate why) and the latest hybrids with the exotic *C.reticulata* in them.

But before wandering through the camellia groves other possibilities are offered. Before the drive, notice some small-leaved evergreen trees beginning to join the high local beech canopy above. These are species of nothofagus from Chile and New Zealand – the overlapping in flora of these two southern hemisphere areas is not unusual. Here, too, is the rare *Magnolia cylindrica* which should be visited in April. Nearby, against the main lawn, is a planting of large monocotyledons – grasses, phormiums, yuccas and so on which are complemented by bog plants at the foot of the southernmost scree.

The drive itself is bordered by more fine plants as it curves on towards the house, whose walls give protection to interesting tender species. By the front door a peculiar member of the Araliaceae, for all the world like a hardy Dizegotheca – at present nameless – offers a plant shape unknown in the open English garden.

Following now back to the Jermyns Lane boundary but keeping west of the drive a vast old sweet chestnut with typically spiralling bark marks the start of the Hillier Centenary borders. This huge planting marches northwestwards across the original 10 acres of arboretum, the borders containing alternate bays of roses and herbaceous plants backed by collections of hollies, conifers and box. The quantity and diversity of material here, as in other parts of the gardens, is truly daunting – or just magnificent if one is willing to take a macroview of the whole.

Beyond the white gate a border of diverse shrubs travels westwards for 400 yards or so and leads to a valley of young acers and a curving, developing pinetum. This may be followed round to return by way of further arboretum developments. Better perhaps is to retrace steps – not all by any means of the plants will have been noted on the way out – to the border's beginning. Now below to the north east a pool is seen with associated plantings of alders, willows and other water-loving species. Follow the signs to the peat garden which should on no account be missed.

A steep north slope is terraced and built up with peat blocks to offer a home for masses of rare species – dwarf shrubs, bulbs and Himalayan plants in particular. This latter theme is taken up into the valley leading up to the back of Jermyns House. It is, in its relative simplicity, perhaps the most satisfying from a garden-design point of view of all the arboretum's diversity. Under tall oaks the banks are planted with choice rhododendrons and associated species to make a truly idyllic picture.

Should this modest selection be insufficient for rabid rhododendron-ophiles, Jermyns Lane can be crossed where in a cleared Scots pine wood the main ericaceous collections are housed. In season these are extravagantly dramatic and anyone with a suitable soil at home can make his personal choice here. This availability of the biggest collection of ornamental trees and shrubs in the world is a benefit that no keen garden visitor to Hampshire should be unaware of. He should be also warned how much time it deserves and intellectual activity it demands. The answer, of course, is to take it as one should any great museum, little and often, season by season.

Hinton Ampner House

S side of A272 Petersfield–Winchester road, 1 mile W of Bramdean village.

The restrained and almost sombre view of Hinton Ampner House which meets the visitor as he drives from the main road either through the park or via the village in no way prepares him for the sunny magnificence of house and garden as he moves round to the south. He may, of course, have been helped by *Country Life* articles or by *A Hampshire Manor*, Mr Dutton's book on Hinton Ampner, but these, and this present short account, can not easily deal with the facts.

In today's terms Hinton Ampner is a large garden – several acres of 'pleasure grounds' and more of walled kitchen garden. Only the latter is old, the rest (as is the house) is a creation of the owner over a period of 40 years and one which must be counted amongst the most successful gardens in the country.

Mr Dutton explains that he has kept in mind Pope's lines on garden-making which are equally relevant to the grand parks to which they referred, to large gardens such as this or the smallest suburban strip:

> 'Let not each beauty ev'rywhere be spy'd
> Where half the skill is decently to hide;
> He gains all who pleasingly confounds,
> Surprizes, varies and conceals the bounds.'

Hence, here the garden is a combination of vistas, enclosures, views and intimate detail.

For all the apparent complication of plan the visitor can make a circumnavigation of the garden seemingly of his own volition but, in reality led by its design. From the forecourt one enters the garden by the east front of the house, centred on a canal shaped pool. Moving forward the first main axis is reached by a broad terrace some 200 yards in length of random-laid rectangular flags extending the full length of pool garden, house and its offices. Planting against the house and below the terrace is luxurious – facing due south the range of plants is extensive with many delightful combinations; purple sage, ligtu hybrid alstroemerias, Headbourne agapanthus. Shrubs and herbaceous stuff mingle. At the west end where traffic is least, thymes, eidelweiss and artemesias romp over the stones.

The next level is a wide grass terrace of even greater length. Enclosed by the retaining wall border and house to the north and yew hedges to the south, over which roses and shrubs peer, one naturally moves westward. A tree-arched vista, past a great worn statue, gives over a ha-ha to the countryside beyond. Eventually a gap appears to the south. Here are mixed borders of shrubs and old-fashioned roses of the Long Walk. This extends the full width of the garden; a procession of Irish yews and eye-catching statues at either end emphasise its length from wherever it is seen.

From here one may either move further south where a curving border of similar luxuriance takes one eastwards or one may turn east at once. Both ways return to the sunken garden on the main north-south axis of the house. Steps lead up to its central bays, steps down give on to a grassy bastion from which unspoilt countryside first falls away then rises up to the distant Downs. A perfect English scene.

East of the sunken garden the planting is more informal, though the strong lines of the design persist. A cross vista has a blue and white porticoed temple to the north with its view down the slope to an obelisk and venerable lime avenue in the park.

Further east is an amphitheatrical croquet lawn with remarkable surrounding planting. A high pleached screen to the south cuts off the country; to the north is a bank of *Hypericum calycinum* topped with a low golden yew hedge while above are silver pear, towering ilex and purple beech.

Moving north east now the Long Walk is crossed and shady walks appear, green and white, box hedges, high philadelphus, yews and hollies wreathed with *Rosa Filipes* 'Kiftsgate' and Russian vine. This almost Regency colouring reaches a cool crescendo in the dell, an old chalk pit whose sides carry the great cartwheels of giant hogweed (*Heracleum mantegazzianum*), *Viburnum tomentosum*, cherries and so on. Hostas, acanthus and astilbes also flourish in this one damp spot.

It is now possible to return to a horseshoe-shaped area called the Yew Garden; this is a simple grass court with an urn and a vast sarcophagus containing, in summer, pink ivy-leaved geraniums.

Back now past the pool to the entrance front and wonders have still not ceased.

An old orchard on the site of the original Tudor house is helped with flowering cherries and bulbs. Its central path leads surprisingly to a walk of calcifuge plants; magnolias, *Rhododendron cinnabarinum* and a few camellias, for here the customary shallow chalky soil is overlaid with a couple of feet of decent loam. The area does not really fit into the general garden plan and its plants are incongruous but no keen plantsman could have resisted the temptation to 'extend the normal range'.

The north drive is now joined with the fine classic kitchen garden on the west; high walls, a broad flagged walk with autumn borders backed by huge old espalier fruit trees and all around beautiful vegetables, their cultivation as impeccable as that of the plants in the main part of the garden.

NOTEWORTHY SPECIES: Too many to list.

Hockley House

On N side of A272 Petersfield–Winchester road, 5 miles W of Bramdean village and 500 yards W of Beauworth crossroads.

The A272 might suitably be termed 'the garden route' as it seems to make available a number of good gardens out of proportion to its importance as a trunk road. Travelling westwards, just past Cheriton crossroads (the Bramdean gardens having been noted) it has to make a swoop to the south leaving in a hollow to the right the fine 1750's red-brick Hockley House. This was once a coaching inn and the straight line of its drive was originally the line of the high-road.

It is now lined with Irish yews and hummocks of box leading to a sweep in front of the house. Views open up across fields to the great beeches which conceal the 'new' road. Here is a small semicircular sunken garden backed by yews and philadelphus; sweet williams are planted to flower at the same time as the latter and provide a combination of scents that would not shame a Chanel.

On the east front, with young pleached limes, an area is devoted to white flowers and grey foliage in tubs and beds. Rose 'Iceberg' tumbles over lavender at its feet.

A pool garden is now entered whose walls and borders have an enviable luxuriance of form and flower. Colours have been kept carefully soft – roses are white and gentle pink planted with peonies, delphiniums and madonna lilies – these latter enjoy the chalky substrate. (The soil is clay with flints over chalk.) Weight is provided with hebes and other shrubby things, whilst walls carry *Solanum crispum*, the lovely white form of *Abutilon vitifolium*, *Hydrangea petiolaris* and *Clematis montana*. The reputably tender New Zealander *Pittosporum tenuifolium* does well in this very cold valley.

A gap in the east wall by the greenhouse leads to a raised border of calcifuge things – rhododendrons and azaleas – with *Photinia serrulata* and *Eucalyptus globulus*, both examples bravely defying the local likely weather conditions, the first with its scarlet spring shoots.

Billowing yew hedges lead towards a tennis court with some interesting new young trees in the foreground; here is a range of sorbus and acer species. *Populus* 'Androscoggin', an American cross of *P.maximowiczii* and *P.trichocarpa*, is making prodigious growth.

NOTEWORTHY SPECIMENS: Mulberry, purple beech.

Holywell House

On W side of the A32, opposite Soberton Mill, 4 miles N of Wickham.

A long tree-lined lane leads up from a bridge over the little River Meon and eventually sweeps up before this good mid-eighteenth-century brick house with its contemporary bays. The south front, suitably unplanted looks away across a ha-ha to fields and vista carved through the once surrounding Forest of Bere. A convenient central oak remains as an eye-catcher in the far distance.

Hence the gardens are at the sides of the house. To the left a curved flagged path leads to an enclosed terraced garden with a central garden-house. Terraces and borders are generously planted with shrubs and large herbaceous things. Colour, texture and shape of foliage are important. The soil is acid clay over chalk and flints.

Returning in front of the house the visitor moves north to an herbaceous border whose wall conceals the stable yard. Here are roses clematis (*C henryi* is a very good white) and two plants of *Drimys winteri*. This unusual Chilean relation of the magnolias flowers well here. Opposite, first is an almost secret herb garden and then a broad grass path leads between two 'potagers' — vegetable plots surrounded by trained fruit trees and formally planted crops — to a rose garden. Good ideas abound; a red rose climbing up a purple maple hangs over a seat, a laburnum screen of alternate standards and espaliers edges the wood.

At the bottom of the slope an urn takes the eye but first a path to the north leads under huge Scots pines into an extensive woodland garden of rhododendrons, camellias and associated plants. Hydrangeas, hostas, hellebores and lilies extend the season at each end. Emerging at the bottom of the wood by the urn which was glimpsed earlier a long curving shrub border leads south eastwards. Cherries give early interest with later shrub roses for strong colour.

A wide pergola is draped with vines and roses — sensibly it is entirely paved — through which a peony garden is seen, brilliant in June.

Hurst Mill

2 miles SE of Petersfield. On E side of B2146, mid-way between Petersfield and South Harting.

To visit X Mill or the Mill house at Y is seldom a disappointment; the site and frequently the buildings are of some antiquity, often vernacular architecture at its best. The presence of water (few are of any other motive power) is invariably an asset and never more so than when used as a vital part of the garden.

Hurst Mill, on the very eastern edge of the Hampshire county boundary if not actually over it, is no exception. Indeed its situation is one of the most beautiful that any garden could desire; it has been used with uncommon care and hence the combination of nature (or at least as close to nature as the South of England can provide) and artifice never jars.

A narrow lane drops eastward from the B2146 canopied by high beech and pines and steeply banked. In two or three hundred yards a gap opens to the right (south) on to the heavily shaded courtyard of the entrance front of the house. Ahead the lane (or drive) passes under a wooden bridge and snakes down to the old mill itself, some way below the house, thus bisecting the garden.

The walls of the entrance paved court apart from that of the house are virtually high retaining walls and from the top, backed by trees, quantities of *Cotoneaster horizontalis* cascade downwards. From inside, growing up to meet it, is a range of things that provides foliage effect at all seasons; *Mahonia x* 'Charity', whose yellow spikes in November echo a nearby variegated *Elaeagnus pungens*; *Berberis thunbergii atro purpurea* contrasts with both and the purple is repeated by an adjacent buddleia in summer. Other good big leaves are provided by Loquat and *Hydrangea sargentiana*; conventional hydrangeas (which are excellent shade plants) flourish under the dark north wall of the house.

At the north east corner entrance is given to the garden proper and, walking round to the south front the full dramatic effect of the site is appreciated. The house (apparently old but in fact of 1929, using old materials) sits on a shelf of a hillside sloping south east and south. Behind and above is the entrance beechwood, to the right are lawns giving on to pasture and chalk downs beyond, while to the left the garden proper falls away to the sound of cascading water. Ahead, dividing country from garden in both fact and feeling is a great lake glimpsed through carefully grouped trees. The effect is stunning not least because it is so unexpected; chalk downs don't harbour such stretches of water.

Concentration can now be given to the immediate garden planting; the east and south terrace is wide enough for really generous groups of maquis-type plants to behave really typically, huge billowing bushes of rosemary, ceanothus, *Senecio greyii* and cistus pile outwards and above the house carries *Magnolia grandiflora* and a marvellously fruitful vine. The terrace is closed at the west by an urn in a yew niche. Above, the rising ground is planted with a range of interesting young trees.

Steps lead to a lower, grass terrace and then again to sloping lawns. Both retaining walls are softened by and protect generous plantings of low shrubs and herbaceous material; roses are predominant on the east side.

The southern steps lead across the lawn to a little stone belvedere above the water and further steps curve down to meet it. Balustrading is draped with *Lonicera japonica halliana* and above is the canopy of a splendid group of trees designed to give maximum autumn effect when seen from the house; willows, *Taxodium distichum*, *Parottia persica* and Japanese maples.

At the lake-edge water is brought in under a small bridge to feed a newly planted water-garden. From here the noise of water becomes omnipresent as the cascade from the lake (which is, after all, a huge millpool) falls by the side of the old mill (the wheel is in place though not working). At this point the group of buildings — mill, garages, cottage — at which the drive culminates, combine with the surrounding vegetation to make a comfortable domestic scene.

A narrow bridge crosses the cascade and the mill-leat fall and leads to a woodland walk on the north-facing side of the now narrowed valley. After a few paces a superbly romantic view back to the mill and lake with the house poised above is obtained. It is accentuated with strong planting at the bottom of the fall — a huge snake-bark maple gives light shade to smaller cherries, bamboos, *Osmunda regalis*, lysichitum, the great round leaves of *Gunnera manicata*.

Ages of leaf-fall have built up a suitably organic soil for rhododendrons and camellias to succeed and clearly the humid microclimate encourages the highly successful growth here and across the valley. Eventually the path descends and recrosses the stream by a huge half-fallen catalpa. Here is an area of informal beds of shrubs and young trees. Choice is eclectic with davidia — the handkerchief tree, unusual birches and maples. Old trees are invariably made to act as involuntary host to other things. At one point a Lawson's cypress and a wild cherry grow close together; a rose now throws its garlands to join them and *Hydrangea petiolaris* is clambering up to cement the bond.

Above the cottage the planting on this south-facing, yet shady, valley side is tighter with rhododendrons – mainly small-leaved species and modern hybrids – being underplanted with hellebores, bulbs and, under a big Scots pine, *Lithospermum purpureo coeruleum*. To the right across the drive a shelf for a tennis court is cut out of the slope with high 'clunch' retaining walls above and below. These are completely clothed. with the roses ('Wedding Day' is vast) that are such a feature of Hurst Mill, and ceanothus.

Inside the upper wall is the kitchen garden which is approached by the wooden bridge spanning the drive that was glimpsed earlier. On its western side a path leads through flowering trees – including a splendid old *Cotinus cogyggria* – back to the east terrace of the house. From here the plants screening the drive on its curving route can be admired both as a dramatic concept and as individuals. Initially this may have been a very big rock garden but now only plants show. At the top around a big *Eucalyptus gunnii* a range of conifers crowds – *Chamaecyparis law-soniana* 'wissellii' with almost contorted blueish shoots is especially fine – and other good plants include *Ozothamnus rosmarinifolius* from Australia, hebes and azaleas for spring colour. *Phormium tenax* and the variegated *Cornus alternifolia* add final punctuation marks at the lower end.

Any one perambulation is bound to omit good plants, well placed, and also fascinating views. Clearly it must now be done again in reverse.

NOTEWORTHY SPECIMENS: Aesculus, weeping ash, *Ginkgo biloba*.

Jenkyn Place, Bentley

Off A31 Alton–Bentley road. Turn N up Crondall road at Bentley village crossroads, for 400 yards.

Here is one of the most exciting gardens in the two counties, full of interest at every season of the year. Excitement comes from its unique combination of maturity and development; all gardeners know that unlike other works of art no garden, however perfect, is ever 'finished' and if it does not move forward it is bound, by the very nature of plants, to go back.

In the 30 years of the present owners' tenure forward movement has been continued, and continues, both by bringing further areas into the grand design, by altering relationships of the parts and of course by planting. The choice for the latter is both eclectic and catholic; that a plant is a good one is the sole criterion.

Jenkyn Place lies on Upper Greensand on the north side of the Wey valley, thus enjoying a warm and protected southern aspect. A steep 'hollow way' lane rises from the village of Bentley and the drive suddenly appears by old oasts (this is still a hop-growing area) and sweeps round in front of the house. The ground falls to the front door, with its shell canopy; curving steps, two up and two down both protect the house from flash floods and provide a stage for a lead cistern planted with *Hydrangea petiolaris* and stone vases. The summer hydrangeas are replaced by shaped yews in winter.

This entrance court is shaded by high conkers, a lime and a ginkgo underplanted with spring bulbs and the walls begin to indicate the extraordinary range of plants to be enjoyed in the garden proper. Here are planted a range of camellias; over an old dog-kennel tumbles *Actinidia kolomikta* with showy pink and white leaf-tips and the uncommon *Mutisia ilicifolia*. This is one of a group of South American climbing composites with showy gazania-like flowers. There are several good vines and on the densely shaded north wall by the garden gate grows *Schizandra grandiflora rubriflora* – interesting in leaf and outstanding in flower.

Through the oak gate, with the house to the left, is the first bit of the garden proper; a 'roofless-room' with doors on three sides. A central boy-with-a-fish fountain is surrounded by *Daphne collina*, tidy of growth and offering two seasons of scented flowers, though the species – like many daphnes – is not long-lived. Scent is always exaggerated by an enclosed garden and here the fact has been used to effect by planting roses, myrtle, a huge prickly *Colletia armata* and white rosemary. Four eighteenth-century lead tubs hold lemon verbena in summer and clipped box in winter. This habit of Jenkyn Place of using seasonal shrubs in containers might be more commonly copied; only a bit of frost-free space (a light garage-end, perhaps) is needed and care to avoid summer drought.

One can now move south through a screen of arches behind the colletia or west along a paved walk. This last is the site of an old orchard and the three venerable apples that remain hold better climbers than crops. Beyond is a croquet lawn of perfect grass with equally perfect yew hedges on three sides. Cross walks appear at once; down the slope the vista is closed by an urn under a large lime; up steps to the right is the rose garden.

A long canal with interesting water plants (note the blue *Pontederia cordata*) is central, four beds contain hybrid tea roses with a western backdrop of huge old-fashioned types. Uncommon species on the walls include *R.bracteata*, *R.banksiae* and *R.fortuneana*. The north wall is made even higher by a backing of cypresses into which has scrambled *Caesalpinia japonica*; this is a must to be seen in June – and just as strongly to be avoided at pruning time; its thorns are prodigious. Other good shrubs against this warm wall are *Carpenteria californica*, (loquat), *Piptanthus laburnifolius* and two unusual buddleias. *B colvillei kewensis* has individual flowers the size and shape of small foxgloves and *B farreri* flowers in spring on bare twigs. The huge felted leaves which follow make a fine feature in themselves.

Returning to the Croquet Walk at its west end the boundary shrub border contain many good things worth protracted study, then you should turn left downhill. A curved stone seat sits in a stage-set of clipped yew and stretching back towards the house a pair of classically perfect herbaceous borders are planted for high-summer effect. Paving edges to the grass walk permit plants to soften naturally formality of design.

High iron gates at the east end balance the stone seat at the west as eye-catchers. By them the evergreen tree is *Photinia serrulata* – a rose relation that bears both reddish spring foliage and autumn tints.

Before reaching the gates the cross vista that was glimpsed from the rose garden is met again. Upwards it is seen to have 15 steps on three levels. Follow it now down through the herbaceous borders backing the southern hedge. It becomes bordered with old apple trees which are in turn underplanted with crinums and agapanthus, neither of these commonly seen either in quantity or as open garden plants with a conscious use. Needless to say, here it works well.

At the end of the path is an old pilgrims' well. In this area, half-shaded by tall limes and several specialist plantings are old-fashioned roses ('Empress Josephine' and 'Gruss an Teplitz' are particular favourites), peonies and lupins. Good occasional pieces of statuary add focal points where needed.

From here it is possible to move in several directions, but first, before irrevocable decisions are made, two or three low steps should be ascended to enter a charming little circular herb garden. Surrounded by scented Penzance briars, it is paved with 'orange segments' removed for planting. In the centre is a winsome French eighteenth-century statue of the young Bacchus.

The areas by the western boundary, until recently kitchen garden, are in the process of development to complement the nearby maturer parts. These new conceptions are, from north to south an autumn and winter garden, a formal garden of contrasting textures and colours (both of plants and inanimate material) centred on a grand armillary sphere, and in the south west corner collections of hollies, *Rosa rugosa* forms and other shrubs. This spot is guarded by a pair of eighteenth-century stone lions.

Moving now eastwards a cool beech-hedge walk with a sleeping lion at its end contrasts with the surrounding plantings. The eastern exit from the beech walk leads to the sunk garden, centred on an enormous Ali Baba jar. Some of the shrubs on the retaining wall and southern bank have reached equally prodigious proportions, notably *Hebe cupressoides* and *Lonicera maackii*.

There is at last now a view to the main south-east front of the house some 250 yards up the gentle slope. Good young plants abound on each side as one walks towards the house. Styrax and pterostyrax, aesculus species, the rare *Cladrastis sinensis*, Judas tree and so on. Jenkyn Place is not a rhododendron garden but a number have been planted in a spinney on the eastern boundary, combined with hydrangeas and other things to extend the season of interest.

Having reached the house terrace the visitor turns to orientate himself; to the west the gates leading to the herbaceous borders and the roofs of the old farm buildings round the entrance garden. The long valley vista up which he has come is now observed to be clearly off-centre from the house façade, a problem of design that has exercised the owners for decades. Note therefore must be made of the siting of the stone seat and its backing to form a logical nearby eye-catcher.

To the east of the seat are some more fine shrubs and trees, notably a specimen of *Magnolia dawsoniana* now over 30 years old with a branch spread of 40 yards circumference and flowering regularly; this species is related to the better known *M mollicomata* and is just as spectacular. It is underplanted with forget-me-nots which give ground-colour as the flowers above begin to fade.

On the house itself is a range of scented climbers, common, such as summer jasmine and Dutch honeysuckle, or unusual and reputably tender such as wattakaka, mandevilla and tracheliospermum. All earn their keep in such a position.

The east front of the house is dominated by an enormous Cedar of Lebanon, one of the largest for its height in the country; it was planted in 1828.

Behind is a further terrace with more good plants. *Magnolia delavayi* is on the wall of the house, there also is a vast indigofera. Nearby *Clematis balearica* flowers in February and also one of the surprising plants that makes Jenkyn Place so remarkable. This is *Acradenia frankleniae*, a Tasmanian seldom – if ever – seen doing so well as here. Throughout, this is a garden to linger in and savour and to visit at different seasons; seldom is such a success made of combining a plantsman's compulsion to keep adding to his collection with an overall maintenance of cohesiveness of design. The acres are, amazingly, kept in a state of near-perfection by a staff of 3, plus, of course, the owners.

June, Seaview Road, Walkford

Off A35 Lyndhurst–Christchurch road, 3 miles E of latter. Turn SE at Hinton Admiral.

When it is seen from the *Yellow Book* or wherever that a 'small garden' is open to public view the phrase is apt to encompass anything up to 10 acres, depending, perhaps, upon the aspirations of the describer.

But here 'small garden' is what it says – about a quarter-acre – which therefore is of particular interest to the majority of visitors whose own plots are of similar size. Here the requirement is to grow a wide range of plants, hence lawn areas are made to reach somewhere, rather than to facilitate games or open vistas. Surrounding borders are mixed – shrubs, roses and herbaceous material. There are good plants of *Eucryphia* x *nymansensis*, *Cytisus battandieri* with its pineapple scented flowers in early summer, and hamamelis for winter interest.

Several small sitting-out areas and a concentrated vegetable patch with prefabricated cold frames indicate the dedicated do-it-yourself gardener. Many grape vines, notably 'Chasselas d'Or', succeed well. NOTEWORTHY SPECIMEN: Mimosa (*Acacia decurrens dealbata*) against the house.

7, Kingsgate Street, Winchester

S of Cathedral and College, E of A33 (Southgate Street) main road S from city.

Of the dozens of gardens opened by their owners in the two counties there can be few where that means that the house has perforce to be open as well. Yet 7, Kingsgate Street adjoining Winchester College is one such, in a street of gracious Georgian fronts stuck, as so often, on to older backs.

No. 7 has an ideal town garden (except that, like visitors, any load of manure would have to come through the front door). It is surprisingly large – a rectangular near half-acre with a part-time gardener and thus therefore rather atypical, yet offers to owners of similar gardens hosts of good ideas. It is also packed with plants; both ordinary (if they are good) and unusual.

The passage through the house leads to what is in fact the first terrace. It has been glassed in and most of the ground area given up to a swimming pool – not, it should be added the usual improbably blue and chlorine-smelling hole – but a forest pool surrounded by exotic shrubs and climbers; orange *Buddleia madagascariensis*, scarlet *Passiflora racemosa*, royal-purple *Tibouchina semidecandra*, Angels-trumpet daturas and so on.

Doors open to the next, this time open, terrace. Steps ascend to the top of a huge central covered rain-water tank (evocative of Jokanaan's cistern in Salome) which is necessary to provide for the many pot and tub plants – mostly lime haters – which crowd every corner. Ground space around the tank is little more than access to further plants yet is itself texturally satisfying with patterns of paving, setts and cobbles. The plants are equally carefully chosen to touch every sense. Cistus and ceanothus give out breaths of maquis, climbers tumble out of shrubs, golden hops from eucryphia and clematis from the rare *Buddleia colveillei* (which has the biggest individual flowers of its genus). A most striking climber in flower is *Calystegia sepium* – but beware, this is the utterly noxious weed bellbine; lovely but lethal. No doubt if the battle has been lost it is only intelligent to make a virtue of it.

A single flagged path now leads between two raised beds with mainly calcifuge plants in prepared soil. *Rhododendron campylocarpum* at this height shows off mahogany flaking bark that *Acer griseum* would be proud of. Underneath is the rare liliaceous shrublet *Philesia magellanica*. We are now in the 'foliage garden', a symphony of greens and interesting shapes. Around a few square yards of grass are massed hostas, acanthus, rheums, *Paeonia mlokosewitschii* et al.

An arch through a high escallonia hedge leads to the third garden designed mainly in soft pinks and blues and purples. Blue clematis grows through *Cupressus arizonica*, a pink one through variegated *Cornus alba*. There are roses, *Hydrangea aspera*, hebes and crinums while giant hogweed towers above one corner.

A thick cupressus hedge would appear to end the garden. But no, a diagonal hole like a squint has been cut to give access to a greenhouse or two and – always necessary but difficult in enclosed town gardens – compost and bonfire areas. Even here there are good plants: vanilla-scented *Azara microphylla* and *Pittosporum tenuifolmum*.

There is, of course, no way back except that through which you have come. No matter; more plants will take the eye, more combinations will need to be jotted down, as views are reseen in reverse.

Visitors to 7 Kingsgate Street not yet sated with good things or merely depressed at the almost inevitable comparative paucity of their own plot should turn towards the Cathedral. In College Street where a plaque marks the house where Jane Austen died in 1816, are fine magnolias, *M soulangeana* for spring and *M grandiflora* for summer. To discover the third of a remarkable trio go now into the Cathedral Close and find on a wall a fine young plant of the rare *Magnolia delavayi* with great grey-green wavy leaves and horn yellow flowers. Of course, with such superb architecture, domestic and ecclesiastic, on every side even the most ordinary plants would take on a certain polish. And they do.

Kings Chantry

Binsted, off A31 Alton–Farnham road. N of Holybourne turn E and at Binsted crossroads S towards church.

Binsted village lies high above the Wey valley and looks down west-

KINGS CHANTRY

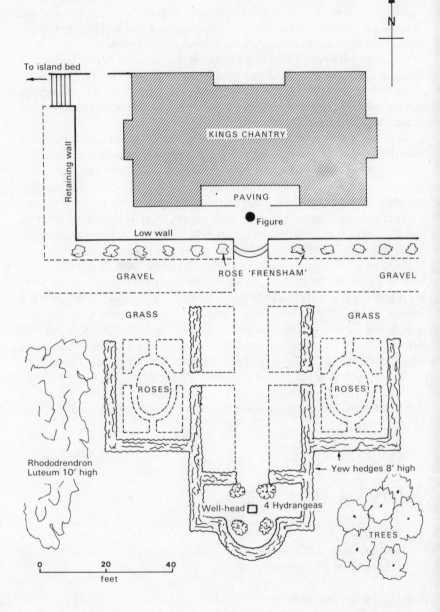

To island bed

Retaining wall

KINGS CHANTRY

PAVING

● Figure

Low wall

GRAVEL

ROSE 'FRENSHAM'

GRAVEL

GRASS

GRASS

ROSES

ROSES

Rhododrendron
Luteum 10' high

Yew hedges 8' high

Well-head ☐ 4 Hydrangeas

TREES

0   20   40
     feet

wards upon it. Kings Chantry gets every wind that blows but mature plantings and high hedges temper them. And with the protection the Upper Greensand soil encourages everything, calcifuge and calcicole alike, to flourish.

A couple of hundred yards of drive, under high *Prunus avium* and a pair of yews, sweeps up in front of the house. The tall surrounding hedge has just solid catmint at its foot, a summer circle of clear blue. A small door leads to the garden, or to be more exact, two gardens though they are not at all separated. Look and turn right and the ground drops away through borders of rhododendrons and azaleas under high trees. Follow the terrace and turn left in front of the house (symmetrical sixteenth-century re-creation of 1911 — before the style was debased by suburbia between the wars). In front is an equally symmetrical rose and herbaceous garden based on yew hedges 8 ft high. The inner two contain the main axial view and wide herbaceous borders; again edges of catmint lead the eye down to an urn and stone seat in a distant apse.

The other two hedges each enclose a formal rose garden and the whole makes an immensely satisfying entity; formal yet lush enough in plant growth to avoid rigidity.

The informal garden contains an island bed which is a garden in itself; towards 50 species growing tightly together to banish all weeds. (The shape unfortunately looks like a foetal tadpole in my plan.) This is worth careful study.

The 2 acres or so of Kings Chantry is maintained impeccably by one man who manages well the difficult art of combining maturity with development.

Lepe House

Exbury, 17 miles SW of Southampton. Take the B3053 from the A35 to Lepe Point, SE of Exbury village.

The gables of Lepe House overhang the sea at the very entrance to the Beaulieu River, to which the garden runs parallel. As this longest side faces south west across the sea to the west, wind protection above the low cliff is of prime importance. This is done effectively and with little contrivance; inside the sea walk a broad band of the native shrub layer has been left – wind-torn blackthorn and sycamore, rose and bramble – inside of which is a high belt of holm oak, Monterey cypress and pine. This makes a shady walk, heavy in summer with the smell of resin. At the end the roof of an old dovecote provides a viewing point for watching the river traffic and wild birds on the Needs Oar Reserve across the estuary.

Behind the house the old kitchen garden holds now a swimming pool. Walls are clothed with camellias and roses. A large collection of peonies give early summer interest, behind which the tender *Jasminum polyanthum* succeeds on a south wall.

On the outside of the kitchen garden walls are other plants of interest; *Lagerstroemia indica*, the crêpe myrtle, on the west and that odd climber *Akebia quinata* on the south. Round the corner a sundial marks (apart from the time) the south end of a long yew walk, closed at the bottom by a statue. From the latter a border of azaleas, overhung with laburnums and cherries, leads to the left. At its end where wisteria climbs into an old 'Kanzan' cherry, is a small sunken rose garden centred on a Romanesque wellhead. Behind is a fine pair of the vanilla scented *Azara microphylla* and a cut-leaved alder. Gates open onto a woodland garden of tall rhododendrons and associated calcifuges.

Little Chilland

Martyr Worthy, 4 miles NE of Winchester, ½ mile W of Itchen Abbas. Signposted 'Chilland' leading S from the B3047.

Here is some three-quarters of an acre of intensely cultivated and cherished garden surrounding its house, which is maintained by its owners and 'half a man'; not a corner is wasted, hardly a plant is not tried. The curving entrance drive is bounded by wide mixed borders, behind which, to the south, is a fruit and kitchen garden area.

Dwarf and medium-sized conifers are a feature throughout but especially in a carefully grouped collection under an old may tree in front of the house. A horizontal cephalotaxus is noteworthy. Further dwarf conifers give permanent weight to an adjoining alpine bed where the stone is, for once, really well laid. Good plants include *Salix wehrhahnii, Lavandula stoechas* and *Daphne collina.*

The main lawn slopes away southward bounded by sweeping borders of shrubs and small trees. Camellias enjoy the shade but by rights should not succeed in this limey soil: they don't, and closer examination shows them to be in plunged tanks of prepared soil. A distinctive conifer in this area is *Cunninghamia lanceolata*, reminiscent of monkey puzzle but without the latter's gloom, rigidity and overtones of mid-Victorian villa front gardens.

Here too are informal beds of roses and interesting specimen shrubs: *Magnolia soulangeana* and *M stellata* do well. West of the house is a little paved area, a garden in itself, presided over by fast-growing young tulip and maidenhair trees. Nearby is one of the most ornamental of Lawson cypresses, especially when its blue-grey leaves are covered with little scarlet male cones; this is *Chamaecyparis lawsoniana cv.* 'Wissellii'. Note, too, contrasting in shape and weight, a Japanese cherry and the flat golden form of *Juniperus media pfitzeriana. Pinus aristata*, the bristle-cone pine from Arizona, also succeeds.

Moving behind the house and emerging by the entrance drive other good borders and unusual plants are found: *Itea ilicifolia* with green catkin-like spikes in August and the variegated hedgehog holly. The perambulation should now be done again to gather up some of what was inevitably missed the first time round.

Little Hay

Burley, off A35 Lyndhurst—Bournemouth road. Turn W at Wilverley Cross. Littlehay is opposite Burley village cricket ground.

One of two adjacent Gertrude Jekyll gardens (the other being Highcroft q.v.). Here, although lacking the amount of professional gardener time it once enjoyed (there is now one part-time man) the charm of Miss Jekyll's small gardens can be clearly felt and most of her plan seems to be extant. Unlike many, it appears that she designed Littlehay in situ — for her friend Lady Isobel Ryder — rather than for a site she never knew, which often occurred. It is, in fact, the sort of design for which she was famed, a sophisticated cottage garden.

Opposite the front door one has already passed a path to the right,

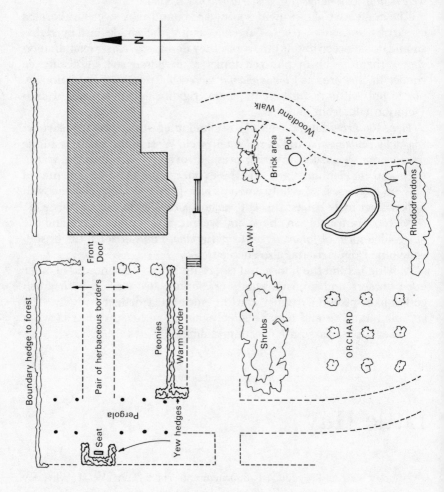

LITTLE HAY

0   20   40

feet

bordered with herbaceous plants and leading, under a pergola, to a seat in a yew niche.

The terrace passes east along the south front of the house — with splendid wisteria on the loggia — and west down three steps to a warm border under a high yew hedge. This leads to the pergola walk through bastions of yew.

A path winds past a herringbone bricked summer-house base, through the orchard. This has good bulbs, narcissus with *Fritillaria meleagris* and wild orchids in season. Following round above a kitchen garden it becomes bordered by a hedge of mixed species. This is a conceit seen at Hidcote; at Littlehay many more things are used: beech, hornbeam, holly, oak and yew with honeysuckle pushing through where it can. Maddening to maintain with all the different growth periods but delightful to see in its varying colours.

The path now approaches the east and end of the terrace past high rhododendrons and, above a little pool, a tear-shaped planting of small shrubs and heathers; the 'cup' is brick paved with a focal-point pot and makes a most satisfying whole.

NOTEWORTHY SPECIMEN: *Cornus mas.*

Little Down,
Hambledon Vineyard

To NW and above Hambledon village on the B2150 12 miles NW of Portsmouth, 9 miles SW of Petersfield. Approached from A3 or A32.

Above Hambledon Village and enjoying views of Broad Halfpenny Down, the eighteenth-century cradle of cricket, the 1900's house of Little Down stands surrounded by chalkland turf, shrub borders and terraces. But agreeable though these are they are not what visitors flock to see. They come because this is also the Hambledon Vineyard and Winepress.

Begun with 1½ acres and 4000 vines in 1952, the vineyard now covers 5 acres and contains some 15,000 grafted vines. The predominant variety is a hybrid called Seyve Villard 5.276. (Seyval) with smaller quantities, to add quality to the wine, of Chardonnais, Pinot Noir and Meurnier. The site which first tempted the owner to grow vines, is very similar to that of the Champagne country; a south-eastern slope and hot, dry, flinty soil. High pH makes necessary applications of sequestrene but even with this addition lime-induced chlorosis is not unknown.

The vines flower in late June and are harvested – if all the imponderables of weather and depredations of birds permit – some four months later. Even with the, for English-grown vines, near-perfect basic conditions, variation in production is frightening; some 14,000 bottles in 1973, the following year there were 3000. However, heartbreaking though this is to the owner and his workers, visually during the summer a Hampshire vineyard on this scale is of continual interest to the visitor. And the wine, a white, resembles perhaps a *Champagne Nature*; other comparisons have been to a Mosel and to an Alsatian wine. Certainly it is delicious.

Longstock Gardens

3 miles N of Stockbridge. From A30 Winchester–Salisbury road turn onto the A3057 and follow Longstock signs.

One of the most difficult garden features to maintain successfully is a water garden, as any owner of a small pool knows only too well. Will the lilies grow so much as to obscure the water? Or at all? Will the blanket weed bury the lot? Will the fish live? So often these appear imponderables which are out of our control; it is not surprising therefore that visitors are always amazed at the Longstock Water Gardens.

A small gate in a high fence off a narrow country lane is the only entrance, a path between high trees suddenly opening out into the broad panorama of the garden. Here is a 5 acre archipelago; islands, large and small are connected by bridges and linked by causeways around which the water in streams and pools imperceptibly moves. Sometimes it is shallow, the fins of monstrous golden carp cutting the surface, sometimes black and deep.

The deep shade and brilliant open stretches are contrived with native trees and exotics which like the damp; *Taxodium distichum*, the swamp cypress, grows predictably well and throws up big pneumatophores (the necessary breathing 'snorkels') from the water. Cut-leaved alder and *Betula costata*, with fine white and suede-green bark, are both good. Ferns sprout from their boles.

Flower colour all round the watersides progresses from March-blooming lysichitum, through primulas, day lilies, astilbes and musks while nymphaeas float on the surface. The whole is like being *inside* one of that series of paintings by Claude Monet on just this theme.

Beyond the water areas woodland is being opened up to provide sites for less aquatic species. A glade holds blue poppy (*Meconopsis betonicifolia*) and the giant white lily, *Cardiocrinum giganteum*, towering towards 10 ft high. The unusual *Stewartia pseudocamellia* actually seeds itself.

Across the road it is now possible to visit other parts of Longstock's 180 acres. All is country house gardening on the grand scale; an extensive arboretum has been recently planted and moving through this with its rare conifers and deciduous trees one reaches areas south west of the house. On the site of old lean-to greenhouses the original back wall gives protection to tender shrubs, cestrum and callistemon, and general encouragement to more usual things.

A great curving lawn with a huge liriodendron is edged by a border in which swathes of ground cover and foliage plants have been planted to give effective visual help to the ever-present problem of maintenance. The planting here is worthy of note.

Finally a walled ex-kitchen garden is reached with its old pergola of arched apples remaining. In one corner a silver garden has been recently planted to which even Mrs Underwood, who, we now feel, virtually invented silver plants, would give commendation.

NOTEWORTHY SPECIMENS: *Magnolia kobus, Liriodendron tulipifera*.

MacPennys, Bransgore

Open throughout the year, weekdays 9–5, Sundays 2–5. Midway between Christchurch and Burley. Turn N off A35 Lyndhurst–Bournemouth road at Hinton Admiral, then right at Bransgore crossroads.

Associated with the nursery where most of the plants one has admired can be bought is a remarkable woodland garden of calcifuge plants.

Being planted in a gravel pit, whose abstraction had been decidedly erratic, the contours are spectacular; steep slopes and minor mountains make it possible to view many areas from above and to admire plants from entirely unexpected angles. The effect can be dramatic; *Cornus kousa* from the air is an extraordinary sight.

There is always something in flower but, although new plantings begin to extend the range, the emphasis is naturally upon the lime-haters. Rhododendrons, often of particular selected forms, are important but so too are other members of the ericaceae – vaccineums, kalmias and so on. Magnolias and camellias do predictably well with fine old plants of *C.reticulata* to be seen. This latter gives indications of the mild climate and many other tender shrubs confirm it. Big plants of the New Zealand tea tree, *Leptospermum scoparium* are spectacular in June.

As one walks about the narrow serpentine ways the unusual plant or the unexpected tree continually appears. Fortunately they are most of them labelled; or a knowledgeable member of staff is about to help with a name that, just for the moment, escapes one!

Merdon Manor

Hursley, SW of Winchester. From A31 Winchester–Romsey road turn N at Standon. Proceed for 2 miles.

Merdon Manor is not easy to find but the search is well worth making. Here is a combination of several unusual garden features any one of which could give the feeling of 'that's just what we need' to the makers of smaller gardens.

Over a cattle grid the drive sweeps past the house to a stable yard with statue centre-piece. All round are large rhododendrons in tubs – the chalky soil here making any normal method impossible. A fine lead cistern is planted with *Arundinaria nitida*, its graceful shape contrasting with the formality of the container. To the left of the stable block is a hedge of the rather tender *Pittosporum tenuifolium*; clearly the exposure here causes it no concern.

Returning now down the drive, from the west forecourt (the house draped with *Vitis coignetiae*) a path leads to a paved terrace on the south front with broad views across a ha-ha to the countryside beyond. Rose borders emphasise the line.

Moving to the west a swimming-pool garden is hidden by high yew hedges. A range of deciduous magnolias provides an early-season reason for visiting the area. Interesting shrub borders conceal the tennis court. In the far south west corner is a tree-hung dell planted with shade-loving species – lilies, hostas, ferns, bamboos and here it can be seen just how rampant *Galeobdolon argentatum* (*G.luteum*) can become.

Back across the drive a couple of broad marble steps lead to a wide vista to the north, arched over by a venerable walnut. Extensive planting of shrub roses to one side gives summer colour. At the end stand a pair of famous early eighteenth-century statues by Roubilliac. They depict the Duke of Marlborough and his comrade-in-arms Prince Eugène and came originally from Glenham in Suffolk.

In great contrast to such sophistication is a traditional creosoted barn raised on staddlestones nearby. How good to see these almost inevitable garden ornaments still used for their original purpose. Opposite the east side of the barn is a heavy door in a wall. To open this is to enter the most extraordinary enclosed garden that can be imagined. In fact this is a second barn, some 10 by 30 yards in size, with the top off, tightly planted to take every advantage of the protection its walls afford.

The door gives first onto an ante-room separated from the main garden by a beautiful iron screen. The area is timbered and draped with Russian vine. Two octagonal raised beds had central umbrellas of the tiny-leaved New Zealander *Muehlenbeckia axillaris*, but this became impossibly vigorous: other unusual plants have taken its place.

Beyond the screen the area is designed as a pool garden with stepped beds against the three walls. These are extravagantly planted with tender climbers – berberidopsis, campsis, passiflora – and the high trees of the park provide a backdrop. These raised areas also make possible camellias, rhododendrons, crinodendron and other calcifuge things which the natural soil precludes. Everywhere pots and urns provide sites for seasonal colour.

NOTEWORTHY SPECIMENS: Yew on south lawn, walnut in the north vista.

The Mill House, Hook

Entrance on main A30 Bagshot—Basingstoke road, 1 mile E of Hook, by Crooked Billet public house.

Inevitably, with such a name the garden here is dominated by water, though not by plants generally associated with it.

The canalized River Lightwater (eventually to join the Loddon before meeting the Thames near Wargrave) flowing northward approaches the south front of the house. Controlled by a sluice much runs underneath, originally driving the mill, the rest is diverted at right angles to pass east of the house. The sound of falling water, therefore, is omnipresent.

Having passed the timbered porte-cochère on the north front of the house, with its fine 'Mermaid' rose, the garden is entered by an arched door. To the left is a small rose garden where clematis 'Perle d'Azur' flourishes on the south wall. The terrace walk in front of the house (lemon verbena succeeds admirably) leads at its west end to a paved path following the water southwards. Passing under two big box elders (*Acer negundo variegata*) roses are planted each side with peonies and helped by seasonal bedding.

Ahead is kitchen garden but a bridge to the left crosses the river. The east willowed bank may now be followed back or a broad walk between wide herbaceous borders. Further east the backing is of old orchard and native trees. Crossing the secondary stream by a brick bridge a bottom border has hemerocallis and iris giving way to native meadowsweet, comfrey and *Veronica beccabunga*, the whole comprising a charming midsummer picture.

Nearby on walls are trained peach and fig trees with quantities of *Iris unguicularis* (*stylosa*) at their feet.

NOTEWORTHY SPECIMENS: *Liquidambar styraciflua* on main lawn.

Michelmersh Court

4 miles N of Romsey. From A3057 Romsey–Stockbridge road turn E at Timsbury for Michelmersh. House is by the village church.

The cool west front of the classically Georgian house, flanked by yew hedges, has been kept – except for wisteria in season – consciously monochrome. The colour and range of plants, in the flanking gardens therefore take on added lustre.

A gate in the yew leads to the south front of the house where the main view from the shell porch is centred upon an armillary sphere and an oak tree in the Churchyard beyond. On the left, above a small pool, a felicitous trio of Irish yew, Japanese maple and bamboo take the eye. Other good trees include taxodium and the remains of what must have been a very large *Arbutus unedo*. Its suckers remain and a replacement has been planted. On the house are passiflora and *Magnolia grandiflora*.

Ground slopes eastward and is gently terraced with brick retaining walls which compliment the house. The wide east terrace is laid out as a formal herb garden – both convenient for use and attractive to view. The pure white salvers of *Carpenteria californica* like a huge-flowered mock orange succeed against an east wall.

The view flows down through trees and meadows to woodland in the valley bottom. To the left a path leads to the swimming pool garden. Here the rectangular pool with a backdrop of trees, roses and trellis has been effectively fitted in to the scene. *Phormium tenax, Vitis coignetiae* and catalpa add strength of foliage and a necessary touch of the exotic.

Leaving the pool below, an open-sided tiled barn with honeysuckles on the supports holds a collection of peafowl beyond which, north of the entrance drive, the mulberry garden (whose name-tree is remarkably tall) has old-fashioned roses and peonies around a white gazebo and a small collection of magnolias. *M.salicifolia*, like a particularly well-grown *M stellata*, is notable. As it has the advantage of scented leaves and bark, it should be grown more.

NOTEWORTHY SPECIMENS: *Liriodendron tulipifera*.

Mottisfont Abbey

4½ miles N.W. of Romsey. From A3057 Romsey–Stockbridge road turn off W at sign to Mottisfont. Abbey entrance in centre of village.

If Hampshire and Dorset are not as rich as some counties in great bespoke country-houses, they have several of the sort which began as monastic buildings and took on secular use after the Dissolution in the sixteenth century. Almost inevitably these possess a beauty of buildings and situation which combines with later garden development to make a most felicitous whole. Mottisfont is no exception.

It was founded as a Priory of Austin Canons in 1201. Although it was never very important the beautifully illuminated Rental Book kept by the cellarer in the 1340's describes Mottisfont in its prime. He lists, amongst other things, two gardens, two courtyards, and an apple yard. Not surprisingly nothing of these gardens remain but their site.

Of the buildings, however, there is much; some visible, some hidden behind the elegant near-Rococo south front remodelled in the 1740's when the first great Tudor house (the Priory had been acquired from Henry VIII by Lord Chamberlain Sandys) was reduced in size. Then after nearly four and a half centuries of private ownership, in 1957, Mottisfont, with over 2000 acres, as well as an endowment, was given to the National Trust by Mrs Gilbert Russell. For much of the garden around the house, dating from the 1930's, the donor and her husband, with various advisers, were responsible. Hence garden design and developments, which still continue, are the product of many ages and attitudes. Yet they provide a certain cohesiveness. The visitor to Mottisfont now arrives at the car park made by the Trust in one of the two walled gardens in the village above, and to the west of the Abbey itself. Two very different choices are now open; to enter the new planting in the second kitchen garden or to go straight down to the main grounds. Perhaps the first is sensible, then, if as may be expected, a second look is desired it can be obtained on the way home.

Through a door in the high brick wall the visitor is suddenly transported (so long as he goes at the right time of year) into a garden of idealised late nineteenth-century or Edwardian lushness. At least that is the atmosphere there. It is, in fact, in its present form only five years old. By great good fortune when this garden became available the well-known collection of old shrub roses that had been brought together over many years by Graham Stuart Thomas (then Gardens Adviser to the National Trust) was needing a home. This amalgam of collection and site is proving remarkable for the old kitchen garden with its box-edged paths was right both in feeling and basic design for the requirement.

Although the intended collection is not quite complete, towards 300 different forms of roses are already here providing, in June, an unsurpassed experience of fragrance and colour. Here are the ancestral species and ancient hybrids – The Apothecaries Rose, damask roses, moss roses. Many of the nineteenth-century variants of these historic roses were cultivated in quantity by the Empress Josephine (Napoleon's first wife) at Malmaison; many too were painted for her by Redouté. Here at Mottisfont his pages live.

Species and forms which enter later into the story of rose hybridisation, the Portland roses, Bourbons, tea roses and hybrid perpetuals, are also here. Because, however, modern hybrid tea roses are excluded the range of colours is softer and gentler and altogether more in keeping with an English country garden, however grand.

The flowering of these early roses is not the continuous show we now expect, so to extend the interest of the garden there are masses of earlier things – aubrietias and polyanthus to start the display, pinks and *Saponaria ocymoides* for low colour as the first roses come out. Then, to continue summer into autumn interest, a long double herbaceous border, broken in the centre by a pool, bisects the whole garden. Naturally the walls, too, are rose-covered in amazing variety.

This is the first treat at Mottisfont. A second door from the car park wall leads to the main carriage drive to the house. At the point at which it is joined the avenue trees change. To the west, up to the gates, are young mulberries; to the east ancient beeches and sweet chestnuts 'crowd into a shade'. Beyond the drive and further down the slope towards the house a spring emerges from the ground. Now channelled and taken circuitously to the river below the house, this is the 'font' of the place-name and a basic reason for the original siting of the Priory itself.

A perfect view is obtained near here of the exquisite south front of Mottisfont Abbey. Here essence of the eighteenth-century Landscape School is predominant with park sweeping almost to the walls of the house. But on approaching, terrace walls are seen to be clothed with roses (note too a fine *Feijoa sellowiana*; this Brazilian of the myrtle family has edible petals) and, between the wings, a small informal parterre of billowing herbs and seasonal things.

On the east front of the house nothing of the gardenesque mars the calm of great trees and the swift-flowing River Test alive with trout. Mottisfont is noted for its trees but especially remarkable here is a giant London plane. Originally two trees which over the last 100 years or so have grown together, it now forms a vast canopy about 35 yards high covering some 1500 square yards. The trunk is 12 yards round at a height of 6 ft. In its shade plays are performed and both actors and an audience of 200 or so are covered.

The north front of the house is so different from the south as to appear a different place. Lord Chancellor Sandys had used the Priory church as well as the domestic buildings for his mansion and here the full north wall of that church plus its truncated tower is to be seen; only the fenestration has changed.

A broad flagged walk follows the house (on its north east corner is one of the rarer climbing hydrangeas, *Schizophragma hydrangeoides*). To the right broad lawns end in a ha-ha with views across the water-meadows of the Test. Ahead at right angles is a broad mixed border shaded by a double lime-walk planted above the retaining wall behind. In spring the ground is carpeted with blue chionodoxa. The paved walk and the limes meet at a paved octagon surrounded by yew hedges and enlivened by urns and a central ornament. Beyond the octagon is a small collection of magnolias which accept the chalky soil. This route returns to the main drive where it meets the house on its west or entrance front.

NOTEWORTHY SPECIMENS: *Platanus x acerifolia*, *Cedrus libani*, purple and green beech, walnuts.

Moundsmere Manor

Preston Candover, on B3046 Basingstoke–Alresford road. 1 mile N of Preston Candover on E side of road.

After the lodges north of Preston Candover more than a mile of private road rises and falls across farmland before the house approach is announced by a sycamore avenue. This sweeps up past high yew hedges (a feature of Moundsmere) to the imposing north front of the house; *Hydrangea petiolaris* is beginning to soften the austere blind fenestration of the recently truncated north wings.

The gardens – some 30 acres in extent – are entered through the yew to the west, guarded by an immense Dawyck beech (*Fagus sylvatica columnaris*). Here is a small spring garden with beds of Kurume azaleas; the clay-with-flints topping of this chalk-down hill making calcifuge plants possible. This gives on to the west front formal garden; roses and a central wellhead presided over by a pillared garden house.

Through the hedge on its south side one meets the axial east-west walk of the garden front extending several hundred yards from urn-flanked gates on the west to the kitchen gardens to the east. In the former area good specimens of all three cedars — *C.libani, C.deodara* and *C.atlantica* grow together for convenient comparison. Here are also the first of the many splendid fruiting trees of *Picea breweriana* for which Moundsmere should be famed; they clearly like the soil and the rather unusually open positions they have been given.

From the centre of the garden front the full exuberance of the grand Edwardian terrace garden can be enjoyed. (It should be stated here, to avoid misconceptions, that the 'Wrennaissance' house, one of the last to be built on such a scale, was based on aspects of the seventeenth-century parts of Hampton Court by Sir Reginald Blomfield in 1910. It also indicates why the fine trees are all in early middle age; they have every indication of maturity without the shadow of senescence. Ahead is a fine sunken canal garden with views to distant hillside beyond. Formal beds, presently planted with roses, surround it. The longitudinal effect is emphasised by parallel lines of clipped yews with, either side, deep herbaceous borders. These are backed with yew and divided every so often with forward-thrusting bastions clipped into the curves of a contemporary Edwardian cornice.

Ascending the steps at the far end of the canal (the retaining walls are masked with clipped escallonia and trained wichuraiana roses) one reaches a viewing platform; again the east-west axis presents itself. Moving eastwards a walk lined with 15 pairs of clipped Irish yews borders a second formal rose garden with its wellhead and garden-house. These latter are more telling than anything else of the age and origins of the garden. Behind it is a big lawn with trees and a long species rose border fronting the kitchen garden wall.

The high old beech woodland to the north conceals and protects a pinetum of formidable complexity planted in the 1930's. Here are many fine species seldom seen outside the national collections: *Pinus montezumae hartwegii, P. x holfordiana* (the cross between *P.ayacahuite* and *P.wallichiana* which originated at Westonbirt around 1906) and *P. ponderosa*. Here too are more 11 yard high specimens of Brewer's weeping spruce. Noteworthy deciduous trees are a field maple (*Acer campestre*) and a fastigiate hornbeam, both beyond their normal size.

From the pinetum it is possible to enter the kitchen gardens on their north side. Some areas have been put down to Christmas trees but the main walled garden with its beautiful curved vinery range (still with good grapes, figs and peaches) is maintained in scale and condition as befits the house and the rest of the gardens.

Norton Manor

Sutton Scotney, 7 miles N of Winchester. Between Sutton Scotney on the A30 and Bullingdon Cross on the A303; ½ mile E of the A34.

The garden at Norton Manor (a charming moated house probably built in the sixteenth century but now giving a general impression of Georgian substance) is best entered by the small door in the wall on the north side. This gives on to a walled rose garden presided over by the Dutch gable of the east front of the house. A large trachycarpus palm set in the lawn looks more than a little incongruous.

A further door to the south enters an elegant ogee-domed conservatory. On the left runs a range of greenhouses where vines, peaches and figs juxtapose with flowers in positively Edwardian splendour. An open-fronted yet covered arch halfway along has a trained pear on one side and, against all the rules, an avocado on the other. Sadly it doesn't fruit yet! This profusion of produce continues to be seen through the panes as a great kitchen garden stretches out.

It is reached through the conservatory whence a flagged path by the side of a wide, rose-backed herbaceous border leads south. At the end a left turn along a lavender walk leads in amongst the vegetables while to the right the south front of the house is reached, dominated by a huge *Cedrus atlantica glauca*. Here is a small formal sunken garden planted with roses and lavenders and a pair of golden yews as focal points. Note should be taken of the necking of the capitals of the brick pilasters on the house; these are uniquely set with yellow and blue Dutch tiles.

Views from this front sweep down to the stream or moat and wide shallow lake. Natural walks with screens of Arundinaria cross and recross the water. Island beds to the west of the house are planted with shrubs and herbaceous material.

NOTEWORTHY SPECIMENS: Atlas cedar, *Chamaecyparis lawsoniana stewartii*.

Oakley Manor

Church Oakley, 4 miles W of Basingstoke, S of the B3400 and N of the A30. Oakley Manor is in centre of village.

The drive sweeps up to this pedimented eighteenth-century house with fine yew hedges while curving walls extend from the house like out-stretched welcoming arms.

On the south side are several unusual garden features; an area of tall trees in cultivated ground underplanted with mature topiary, for all the world like a giant's informal bedding scheme. In line with the south front of the house the view opens up to the country beyond, framed by trees. An unconventional pool lies to one side, its farther water lapping the brick retaining wall of rising ground behind. Climbing *Hydrangea petiolaris* is thus surprisingly seen doubled by mirror image. The huge leaves of gunnera and other waterside plants add further interest.

Five steps lead to an upper lawn from which a walled garden on the west front can be reached. This quiet enclosure has a rose roundel of six beds.

The Old House, Rotherwick

5 miles NE of Basingstoke. Turn W off A32 Reading–Odiham road 2 miles N of Hook. The Old House is in lane leading S from village centre.

This is not a plantsman's garden, full of rare things, but one of space and repose with which it is easy to identify. A gravel entrance court is separated from the road (itself little more than a tarred farm lane) by a timbered cottage range. Barns and the west end of the house, enclose it on two further sides.

South of the court a broad lawn with fine indigenous trees drops to an informal pool edged with primulas. Yellow candelabra, *P.prolifera* does particularly well. On the lawn's eastern edge the boundary shrub border

THE OLD HOUSE

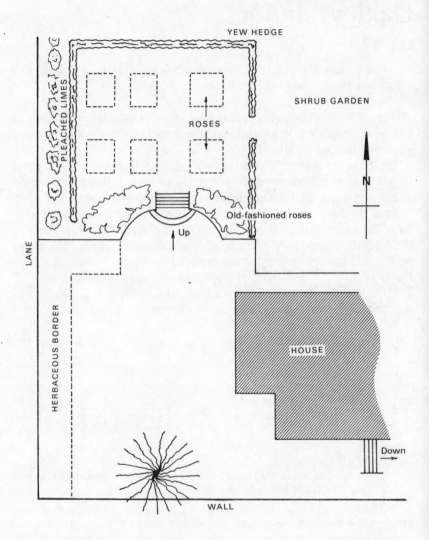

YEW HEDGE

SHRUB GARDEN

PLEACHED LIMES

ROSES

Old-fashioned roses

Up

N

LANE

HERBACEOUS BORDER

HOUSE

Down

WALL

0   20   40
feet

is low enough to see what appear to be hazel plantations in the adjoining fields; much more surprisingly they are witch hazel, *Hamamelis virginiana*, grown for medicaments; surely one of the most unusual field-crops in this country.

The heavy clay here permits a border of hardy hybrid rhododendrons and encourages the roses which are a feature of the garden. North of the house the ground is on three levels, an upper rose garden enclosed to concentrate the scents with 10 ft high beech hedges and pleached limes; small beds of hybrid teas and great billowing heaps of hybrid musks such as 'Buff Beauty'. *Buddleia alternifolia*, flowering at the same time makes an effective complement.

Steps fall to a lawn with a broad south-facing herbaceous border. Roses are added to give weight to the peonies and delphiniums and grey foliage.

NOTEWORTHY SPECIMENS: Apricot on the south wall of the house.

Old Rectory, West Tytherley

---

6 miles SW of Stockbridge. Turn S off the A30 4 miles W of Stockbridge at West Tytherley sign.

A garden of great charm, both in general and, at plantsmanship level, in particular. The shady drive no longer sweeps to the west front of the Old Rectory as it did. Instead its original turning circle has been hidden behind a yew hedge and made into a pool garden, framed by a high stepped rock bank facing the house. The pool itself is shaped like a fan with a flat base; a surprising outline, but one that here fits the enclosed site and successfully combines those almost irreconcilables – the formal and informal – into a cohesive whole.

Grey plants soften the house well: helichrysum, *Ballota pseudodictamnus*, cistus and hebes. *Senecio leucostachys* scrambles through other things.

The rock bank at its south end devolves into a great bed of rock-roses – these do particularly well on the chalky soil – which in turn becomes the formal south terrace. The visitor should now descend the steps and cross the lawn to the groups of shrubs at the boundary before looking back.

The charm of the house – a three storey red-brick block of five bays with no parapet, but early eighteenth-century and in perfect proportions – is now fully seen. Lavish planting on terrace and house walls makes the rather severe building, built on a terrace podium, sit tightly and comfortably into its place, framed by a backdrop of mature trees.

In this far area (the whole is only 3 acres maintained by one gardener and the owner) sweeps of spring bulbs are replaced in season – no unnecessary over-tidyness here – by wild cowslips, buttercups and ox-eye daisies (I even liked on the lawn erring cushions of *Hieracium pilocella*).

North west of the pool garden one wall of a complicatedly rhomboidal kitchen garden is seen. Much still fulfils its original role but from both entrances wide mixed borders of old-fashioned roses ('Fritz Nobis' and 'Queen of Denmark' with quartered flowers are favourites), peonies and irises are seen.

A corner of the walled garden is given over to a small nursery of alpine plants. These are the owner's speciality and quantities are sold to benefit the charities for which the Old Rectory is opened.

NOTEWORTHY SPECIMENS: Huge *Cedrus atlantica* in field east of the house, *Rosa banksiae* on the west wall, mistletoe growing on *Cotoneaster horizontalis*, also on the west wall.

The Old Rectory, Winchfield

2½ miles NE of Odiham. From A30 Hartley Wintney–Hook road turn S on to the B3016 towards Odiham. At Winchfield Station turn E under railway bridge and then first right to Winchfield Church. Drive by the church gate.

A long oak-fringed drive sweeps up before the Gothicised house of warm Caen stone. The garden is mainly based upon mixed borders, in which interesting foliage plays a predominant part, and broad views into the surrounding fields and woodland.

In the north lawn grows an interesting buckeye (*Aesculus sp*). Its contorted branches and surrounding vine-patterned iron seat provide a focal point. The main garden however is to the south, beyond the front door sweep. It is approached through a hedge of *Chamaecyparis thyoides*. Two arms of mixed border spread out from the house, separated by impeccable lawns. To the left, backed by a screen of bamboos, groups of foliage shrubs — *Acer palmatum*, vertical junipers and grey santolina — provide a frame for a marble bust of Lord Cardigan, of Light Brigade fame (or infamy). From here a fine viewing point has been made by driving a vista through the woods. It is conveniently closed by a distant oak and framed by architectural gates.

Returning towards the house a swimming-pool garden is enclosed on three sides by an interesting tapestry hedge of grey Lawson's Cypress, vivid green *Thuja plicata*, darker yew with an admixture on one side of Portugal laurel. All are formally clipped. Behind is an enviable kitchen garden.

The Old Vicarage, Burley

4 miles SE of Ringwood. In Burley village take Chapel Lane turn to Burley Church; house is first on right.

Habitual visitors of Hampshire's gardens over the last two decades will remember with pleasure Brigadier Nicholson's fine achievement at Coles at the top of the Meon Valley. On a smaller scale, but equally impeccably maintained (one acre, one gardener, and only, in 1975, five years old) the Old Vicarage continues to emphasise an overriding interest in rhododendrons, both species and recent hybrids.

A wide lawn of near bowling green quality is surrounded by calcifuge shrubs to which the great oaks of the Forest provide a cooling backdrop. Worth noting particularly for small gardens is the end bed of *R yakusimanum* and some of its hybrids (of which none, to my mind, really improves upon the parent). These tight nummocks, good in leaf in and out of flower are interplanted with heathers and lilies; *Acer palmatium dissectum purpureum* provides contrast of foliage and texture. This is an entirely successful association of plants.

In the main borders the use of *R.yunnaneuse*, a delicately spotted blush pink and the blue *R.augustinii*, both of thin open habit disposes of people who, only knowing ponticum decry all rhododendrons in one derogatory breath. Amongst others of merit rhododendron 'Repose', a fine waxy white, and a *Rhododendron dicroanthum x catawbiense* cross are worth noting.

The highly scented 'Lady Alice Fitzwilliam' indicates the mild winter climate, as do good plants of *Crinodendron hookeranum*, the Chilean lantern tree.

NOTEWORTHY SPECIMENS: New Forest oaks.

Palace House, Beaulieu

At head of Beaulieu River, 10 miles SW of Southampton. Well signposted from the A35 and from A337 Lyndhurst–Lymington road.

Gardens at Beaulieu, rather naturally, are a secondary feature to the great National Motor Museum complex with its displays, motorail snaking through the trees, restaurants and family amusements. All these however are now separate from the house and monastic ruins where plants fulfil their traditional role.

In spring, between the Museum and Palace House are large areas of bulbs under tall trees and a waterside walk follows the edge of Monks Mill Pond. This emerges on the west front of the house; broad lawns, mixed shrub borders and seasonal bedding provide a traditional setting.

In the centre of the Cistercian Abbey ruins (founded by King John in 1204) the well-preserved cloister has recently begun to be laid out as a herb garden – culinary, medicinal and ornamental species make a fine foreground foil to lichened old stone walls. A herb shop adjoins. Also worth investigating is the recently established vineyard. At present under 10,000 bottles per annum are produced from the Reisling Sylvaner grapes but with maturity twice this number should be possible.

NOTEWORTHY SPECIMENS: *Araucaria araucana* with cones west of the house. *Cupressus sempervirens* in cloister.

Pennington Chase

Lymington. Take the A337 W from Lymington and turn S into Lower
Pennington Lane after 2 miles.

Some 2 acres of garden to the south of the mid-nineteenth-century
house is evocative of a contemporary period of garden design. Seasonal
bedding and roses surround a pool, mixed shrubs and trees share a
number of irregular beds and provide interest over a long period of the
year. Surrounding conifers give shade and textural background. On the
house *Jasminum primulinum* (west side) and *Clianthus puniceus* − the
lobster claw − (east) are worth seeing in flower.
NOTEWORTHY SPECIMENS: *Cedrus atlantica glauca, Pinus radiata, Davidia
involucrata.*

Pylewell Park

2½ miles E of Lymington. Take southmost road on E side of Lymington
River by Pier Station.

The gardens of Pylewell Park (the plural may legitimately be used) can
be enjoyed on at least two distinct levels. As a rhododendron collection
of historical and botanic interest, scenically superb in its season, and
also as a more general garden of great charm.
   The site is favoured; within sight of the sea, the hills of the Isle of
Wight rising beyond, it is yet protected by thick plantings of ilex and
Monterey cypress where natural oak woodland does not exist.
   Visitors usually begin by the old kitchen garden on the outside west
wall of which various camellias, notably *C.reticulata* 'Captain Rawes',
flourish. Here too is a small summer garden of old-fashioned roses,
peonies and herbaceous plants.
   Moving south an enormous holm oak (*Quercus ilex*) marks the start
of the woodland garden. Here mown grass paths wind through specimen

plantings of magnolias, dogwoods, arbutuses and a whole range of classic garden shrubs and trees. Many are enormous and could well cause visitors to return home worried at the space they have alloted to similar species. Several eucalyptus tower above the woodland edge, a fine *Photinia serrulata* combining rosy young shoots and scarlet old foliage at the same time is 20 ft high and as much across. *Parottia persica* is a tree.

A broad walk now slopes eastward downhill and gradually widens to give views through the native trees and somewhat incongruously through tall trachycarpus palms as well.

Now appears a great lake stretching away southwards until it is separated from the sea only by a tree-lined strand. At this north end marginal planting of lysichitum (in summer only the heaps of giant spinach-like leaves indicate how good it must have been in March and April), hostas, rodgersias and astilbes extend the season of interest. Quantities of royal fern (Osmunda) and gunnera grow together like a horticultural personification of Beauty and the Beast.

Across a small stream the ground rises and on this ridge are the main rhododendron plantings. As these were begun in about 1900 many of the plants are of full tree size and their contorted trunks add a further beauty to the scene; these plants pre-date by 20 years those at the better known Exbury some 10 miles to the east. There are huge camellias, too, of a similar age.

Returning to the lake one may take the path that follows its banks for a mile or so through bluebells and other native flowers left unmown. Halfway back on the west side a glade opens and following this uphill through further rhododendrons, mainly species (the nearly fastigiate white-flowered arboreums are particularly fine) and early hybrids, the woodland meadow is reached again.

Having found the kitchen garden again a belt walk bordering the park leads towards the house. On a south-facing wall by the swimming pool many tender exotics flourish – prostanthera, the mint bush, bottle-brushes, Chinese persimmon and a huge tree of *Magnolia delavayi* with splendid corrugated bark. This is very much a Hampshire plant; but Pylewell's takes the prize of any seen.

Further, a shady walk is lined with a wide range of camellias which eventually give onto the main south front of the house. The formal parterre is now planted with grey-leaved shrubs and roses around fine Chinoiserie urns. Climbers on the house include both the usual lavender-coloured and white wisterias which reach the full three storey height to the eaves. This 40 acre garden is maintained by two and a half men.

NOTEWORTHY SPECIMENS: Too numerous to list.

Ropley Grove

Nr Alresford, 8 miles W of Alton. From A31 Alton–Winchester road turn SE at Anchor Inn and continue 1 mile on Petersfield road. From the A32 turn W at Ropley–Petersfield crossroads. 2 miles S of East Tisted.

An uncontrived garden of quiet but considerable charm. From the garden front of the house (dated 1742 on the porch) the ground rises strongly in a series of broad grass terraces some 50 yards wide. They are linked by ramps not steps. High trees and undergrowth line both sides through which deeply shaded walks can be taken.

At the top grass becomes less shorn with naturalised bulbs amongst mature woodland which contains a large rookery. A gate gives immediately onto arable fields.

The parallel kitchen garden can then be taken down the hill. At its highest point it is demonstrated again how difficult it is to site a swimming pool in a way that makes it an advantage to the garden as well as to the inhabitants: screening shrubs have grown surprisingly quickly on this chalky soil.

NOTEWORTHY SPECIMENS: *Cedrus deodara, Garrya elliptica, Juniperus* 'Blauws variety', extremely fine Scots pine.

Rotherfield Park

4 miles S of Alton Gates on W side of the A32 in East Tisted village.

At the start of the long curving drive from the model village of East Tisted to Rotherfield Park the house is seen as a distant castellated pile. As one approaches it becomes more, not less, amazing with turrets, towers and balustrades. It is superb in the best Schumanesque Manfred tradition of romanticism all set in perfect English parkland not 10 miles from Jane Austen's Chawton.

The gardens do not disappoint, though gardening of all art forms is in

some ways the most transient. Plants die, or, sometimes more embarrassingly they live to overpower their neighbours in size and vigour. So
here, contemporary with the 1840's house, are great trees: cedars,
taxodiums, superb sweet chestnuts with their typically twisting bark
and enormous yew hedges which are only now gradually, yet firmly,
being cut back hard to their original size.

From the east front which faces the drive ground slopes, below a
retaining wall, in pasture to the village, whose church tower makes the
focal point in the whole composition. Borders round the house and along
the Gothic loggia have several plants of note. *Actinidia kolomikta* colours
particularly well.

But the garden proper begins high above the house, on a level with
the tops of its towers. Here the visitor is transported back into country
house gardening of decades ago: standard cordon apples on the walls,
fan shaped apricots under glass.

From the greenhouses the visitor reaches the big walled kitchen
garden; a garden-house of 1889 looks down wide herbaceous borders
whose traditional espalier apple backing has recently been effectively
replaced by beech. A sundial marks the central cross vista but the main
view continues to a break in the wall with high piers and magnificent
wrought-iron gates.

Beyond, the vista continues through an avenue of yew hedges with
exclamation marks of golden yew every few yards. Turn immediately
right through another iron gate and you are in the rose garden. A simple
rectangle bordered by the 15 ft of soft blue-pink brick wall on one side.
There is a small central pool but interest is concentrated in the roses,
mainly old-fashioned or of shrub type. Brick is also used for the paths.

Beyond these formal areas shrub borders hold interesting species,
their range indicating the odd mixture of soils on these chalk ridges. In
some parts rhododendrons do well without artificial help and hydrangeas
blue naturally. One is surprised (as one is in some Cotswold gardens
equally high and cold in winter) to see excellent specimens of the
Chilean tree mallow, *Abutilon vitifolium*.

Although the main lawns are gang-mown by the farm staff (or even
by the owner) it is salutory to realize that this extensive area with its
highly time-demanding greenhouse is managed by a husband and wife
team with little extra help.

NOTEWORTHY SPECIMENS: Sequoias, sweet chestnuts, *Taxodium distichum*
(fruiting), *Pyrus salicifolia*.

Sherfield Court

4 miles NE of Basingstoke. 1 mile S of Sherfield on Loddon village on W side of A33 Basingstoke—Reading road, by the village church.

The gardens (and the plural may here legitimately be used) at Sherfield Court offer an extraordinary range of interests and experiences.

The drive is shared with Sherfield on Loddon church whose over-restored exterior belies its actual age, and sweeps east in front of the house; the way in which cars can either pass to the garage or reach the door is worth noting. For both house and garden are predominantly to the design of Gerald Wellesley, the architect (later 7th Duke of Wellington who lived here before succeeding to the title).

This south-south-east front has every appearance of the late eighteenth century (though it was much altered in the 1920's and 30's); roof behind a parapet, a blind attic storey and semicircular brick bays at each end. It carries big plants of purple vine and green *Vitis vinifera*, choisya, *Cytisus battandieri* and an embarrassingly vigorous cotoneaster — probably *C.floccosa*. The gravel sweep is virtually here a broad terrace overlooking tree-lined lawns dominated by a big horse chestnut. Fifty year old plants of *Picea pungens glauca* and *Cedrus atlantica glauca* of near similar sizes emphasise how much better a garden plant the latter is if space is available for its ultimate development. They are very close in colour. To the left of these specimens is an herbaceous border which fronts the brick and flint kitchen garden wall. By the house are three fine *Prunus subhirtella pendula* and also a trio of standard wisterias.

Moving east under a big box elder (*Acer negundo*) with *Hypericum calycinum* as ground cover a different scene is encountered. Through an arched door in a high wall is a near-square luxuriantly planted pool garden. The walk ahead to a further door is lined with an avenue of old standard roses, underplanted with *Vinca minor*. Such roses seldom look anything but artificial in the garden scene but here, springing from an evergreen base with a strong background of other things, they are entirely effective. To the right, in front of the wall (a gate halfway down leads to a pair of kitchen gardens) a very broad shrub border holds many interesting things well combined; *Azara microphylla* and *Viburnum x bodnantense* make a good late winter duo. Further round *Cotinus coggygria atropurpurea* conjoins superbly with *Clerodendron fargesii* in fruit; calyces of the latter exactly mirror the leaves of the former.

The high wall ahead of old farm buildings holds *Rosa banksiae* and *R* 'Mermaid' and turning left along it the rectangular pool (ostensibly for swimming but designed for architectural effect, avoiding the now almost obligatory azure interior) is approached with its Irish yews at each corner. The pool, in a lawn setting, is a couple of feet lower than the surrounding walks, the retaining walls planted with alpines and bulbs. Mature shrub borders front and clothe the other two walls.

From a door in the north west corner a small court is crossed. At the corner of a low building a vast Lombardy poplar avenue strides westwards; less than 50 years or so in age, it seems to have acquired a peculiar antiquity. Perhaps this is in association with the site for, turning about, a venerable moat surrounds an island of some 50 yards square. This is overshadowed by the spire of the church but dominated more by the north front of Sherfield Court, no longer Georgian but black and white timbered. Flanking wings end in thatched octagonal pavilions, added in 1922, the far one rising sheer from the moat, a most romantic conception.

Approach to the terrace follows the wall of what was once a staff wing, planted with thriving camellias; they seemed, some years ago, to positively revel in the fire that took the original thatch off this building. They are also in imported lime-free soil. The terrace itself is an interesting and calculated combination of materials; steps from the house, flanked with massed hydrangeas and camellias, drop to a broad area of broken flags (what in a lesser context would be derisively described as 'crazy paving') made architecturally valid by enclosure in formal paving and enlivened by cobbled hexagonals in brick surrounds. Further steps ahead descend to a landing-stage at the moat edge; legitimately yet unusually it is lined with scented-leaved bog myrtle.

To the left a honeysuckle-swathed wooden bridge crosses to the island. Here old fruit trees, often hung with mistletoe, have been interplanted by ornamentals particularly chosen for their autumn tints; *Rhus typhina*, liquidambar and various cornus and acer species colour well. At ground level there is a near 12 month pageant of naturalised bulbs from snowdrops and daffodils through *Tulipa saxatilis* and fritillaries to martagon lilies and, in autumn, forms of *Colchicum speciosum*.

The broad grass ride which surrounds the moat is bordered by mixed shrubs and herbaceous plants and is overhung by great oaks. Surprisingly this watery site is seen to be the highest spot around; ground falls to meadows all around and clearly the springs that arise here encouraged the mediaeval inhabitants to construct this protective pound for their stock and, perhaps, themselves. In all directions, outwards and back to the house, views are good. Particularly fine as a composition (sadly made possible by the loss of great elms in the church-yard) is the spire, east pavilion, backing cedar and cypresses all repeated in the still waters of the moat.

Shotters Farm

Newton Valence, 6 miles S of Alton. From A32 Fareham–Alton road turn E at 'Horse and Groom', 1 mile N of East Tisted.

A garden of some 5 acres created around an attractive farmhouse and its barns from 1967. Planting is imaginative yet restrained which emphasises the importance of the fine old trees with which the site is endowed.

Shotters farm stands 650 ft up on the chalk downs near Gilbert White's Selbourne. Views of the surrounding countryside which drops away to the south and west give indication of gardening potential; lush deciduous woodland with a superb herbaceous layer of bluebells, primroses, anemones and violets and, where arable cultivation occurs, the material that makes this possible – a heavy, alkaline clay-with-flints.

Hence, reflecting the countryside, spring emphases are massed narcissus and other bulbs under developing prunus, in soft pinks and white, and *Sorbus aria* – the whitebeam of the local beech escarpments.

Summer interest is more formal, based upon roses and linked by island beds of mixed shrubs, through which curves an iron-hooped rose pergola covered with 'Caroline Testout'. Foliage effect is important. A surprising success are the groups of rhododendrons and azaleas, ericas and camellias. Here the soil has been augmented with copious amounts of organic matter and, what is so often decisive in the success of the ericaceae on a basically limey soil, equally copious water in dry periods.

Ornamental water, too, is important at Shotters Farm; a large butyl-lined (though not butyl-showing) pool with a pretty neo-Georgian garden-house reflected in it, now replaces an obtrusive tennis court. Nearby is a splendid *Acer campestre*.

NOTEWORTHY SPECIMENS: *Viburnum carlecephalum, Prunus serrula.*

Soberton Mill

4 miles N of Wickham on the A32 midway between Wickham and Droxford.

From the busy A32 the fine old mill and Millhouse stand up above the River Meon amongst willows and other indigenous plants. Only swathes of daffodils in spring make a concession to the gardenesque; more would detract from the scene.

Hence contrast with the impeccable grounds behind the house is the more apparent. These are divided along the contour by the canalised mill leat which, as the flow virtually ceases in summer, contains water lilies. A central vista at the back of the house leads up between a pair of late-summer borders to woodland beyond. Trellis conceals kitchen garden to the south, and a rose garden to the north. Beyond, lawns with specimen trees slope back down towards the leat. A shady border makes possible a range of calcifuge plants which is rather surprising within yards of one of England's classic chalk streams.

Across the leat a bank of shrubs chosen to give interest over a long period, hides the garden from road and river below. Rose 'Aloha' is a particularly favourite. *Eucalyptus gunnii* (occasionally beheaded to keep it bushy) is grouped with purple *Acer palmatum* and huge *Euphorbia wulfenii* to make a splendid picture.

NOTEWORTHY SPECIMENS: Aged wisteria on the house. *Cedrus atlantica glauca* planted in 1938.

Somerley

3 miles N of Ringwood. Turn W off A338 Ringwood–Salisbury road at Ellingham.

Visitors to Somerley expecting to look inward on conventional gardens will be disappointed; those able to enjoy wider concept of garden and landscape will be entranced. The great house built by Samuel Wyatt in 1792–3 has mid-nineteenth-century additions and crowns a steep bluff above the broad plain of the Avon. The once intensely cultivated Italianate terraces, lined with balustrading and urns, now frame, more simply, spectacular views to east and south as the river and its carriers, glinting and sparkling through huge parkland trees, flow down to Ringwood and beyond.

Good plants are not wholly lacking. The south colonnade carries wisteria and *Rosa banksiae* while on the west is a good white laptospermum, sharing a corner with the Brazilian *Feijoa sellowiana* with its edible petals tasting of sugar icing. Two big *Eucalyptus gunnii* guard the west drive and a belt of shrubs is worth careful examination for unusual things. *Stewartia pseudo-camellia* flowers there well.

Sparsholt Manor

3 miles W of Winchester. From A272 Winchester–Stockbridge road turn S at Littleton crossroads to Plough Inn. Entrance is opposite.

A circular drive with large laburnums fronts the 1920's tile-hung house and the attractive basic design of the garden to the south of the house might have been taken straight from Sudell or other books of that period. It still has much to teach us.

From the drive a small rose garden and pool garden are hidden by good thuja hedges. The south front of the house is flagged with a sun loggia at each end. Water falls into a tank below the terrace retaining wall and flows into a circular pool via an 18 in. wide runnel. Views ahead are across open farmland. To the west a pergola at right angles to the terrace, draped with roses and wisteria, leads to a pretty gazebo with an ogee roof.

NOTEWORTHY SPECIMENS: Cut-leaved beech, espalier apples in kitchen garden.

Spinners

Boldre, $1\frac{1}{2}$ miles N of Lymington. From A337 Brockenhurst–Lymington road turn E for Boldre; cross Boldre Bridge; just short of Pilley village turn S into school lane.

Of the 3 acres here two are intensively cultivated and these exclusively by the owner; this provides an interesting (and indeed salutary) model of what can be achieved. The site, mature oak woodland on poor acid soil, lies high above Lymington River and drops westward towards it. Surprisingly cold air does not drain away as well as might be expected and hence Spinners seems particularly subject to late spring frosts.

Nonetheless it is full of good plants, well used. The drive is bordered on its left with recent plantings of the smaller rhododendrons and azaleas. An informal hedge of *R rubiginosum* to the right marks the start of the garden proper, below which a broad grass path sweeps northwards with the ground falling away to the west.

Here are fine young specimens of *Cornus kousa chinensis* and the Chilean firebush, *Embothrium lanceolatum* in its 'Norquinco Valley' form. This is so nearly deciduous as to be far hardier than generally admitted. In this area selected rhododendrons flourish; the yellow 'Crest', cream 'Idealist' and 'Naomi' are particular favourites. Other beds hold a large *Eucryphia x intermedia* and just by the house *Acer pennsylvaticum erythroclada* with its scarlet twigs for winter effect.

Balance between luxuriance of growth, variation in texture, the wish to provide interest at all seasons and an avoidance of confusion is carefully kept. Ground cover is used sparingly (*Cornus canadensis* does enviously well) in conjunction with mulching.

The top path leads down to a shallow dell with hellebores succeeded by massed candelabra primulas as the seasonal showpiece. Hostas, meconopses and quantities of struthiopteris fern contrast. *Magnolia wilsonii* is especially rewarding in June.

Moving round to the front of the house the walls and the bay provided by two wings provide sites for a number of exciting plants. A fine *Lapageria rosea* is on the north wall, with the huge *Geranium maderense* at its feet. Below the terrace is a rock bank backed by high leptospermums and on the other side a late summer border in which self-seeding agapanthus are a feature. A walk further down the slope leads through a copse of temporary Norway spruce amongst which a range of eucalyptus have been planted since 1964. The largest are now real trees of 30 ft or more.

Returning to the house terrace at its southern end, a pool offers positions for more good primulas and other marginal plants. All round at Spinners are worthwhile things, often in particularly good forms; no one genus (not even rhododendron) has been entirely given its own way. Many are being propagated and visitors can come away with the spoils.

Sutton Manor

On W side of A34 Winchester–Newbury road on the S edge of Sutton Scotney village.

Battlemented hedges by the side of the busy A34 point the drive to Sutton Manor. This winds through sweeping lawns of baize-like smoothness under fine trees, exotic and indigenous. The house, entirely veiled in Virginia creeper is another greenness amongst the greens. So strong yet peaceful is all this that any 'garden' in sight is in danger of appearing irrelevant.

Hence colour is kept enclosed, away from the house to the west a walk through a small rose garden leads to a kitchen garden. Walls are tile-roofed (simpler walls in this area are thatched) and laden with trained fruit. Return by the Manor and to the north west are involved retaining walls and terraced beds. Some hide a sunken tennis court and a swimming pool backed by pergolas of roses and honeysuckles. Beds are filled with bright shows of seasonal subjects.

A lower kitchen garden which leads to the estate office is bounded by high yew hedges and wide herbaceous border. Quantities of cutting flowers add to the display.

Tichbourne Park

2 miles S of Alresford. Drive gates on B3046 midway between Alresford and Cheriton.

Nestling deep in the complicated headwaters of the River Itchen (which rises at nearby Cheriton), Tichbourne possesses a site of considerable charm from which the famed Tichbourne Dole is annually distributed.

Broad lawns spread from the east front of the house; shrubs and ornamental trees underplanted with spring bulbs lies beyond in a wilderness intersected with cut rides. The river on this side is broadly canalised, the still wide water then cascades constrictedly beneath an ivy covered bridge. A riverside walk leads up the canal under venerable oaks to an island approached by a wooden bridge.

Below the cascade the stream then makes the southern boundary to the grounds, part entering them again to feed a rectangular moat on the west front of the house. One feels that the buildings should be inside it, instead of which is a lawn with a roundel of roses; hebes, santolinas and ornamental sage hang over the brick retaining walls.

NOTEWORTHY SPECIMENS: *Aesculus hippocastanum* (horse chestnut) on the east lawn.

Tunworth Old Rectory

5 miles SE of Basingstoke. 3 miles E of Basingstoke turn S off the A30 at Tunworth sign, or west off the A32 at South Warnborough.

Way up on the chalk downs south of Basingstoke the tiny church of Tunworth hides behind deep screens of trees. The Old Rectory adjoining is in complete contrast. It is a small English country house with all that the term implies, with a splendid mix of roof lines as it stands in its sweeping parkland and lawns. Most of the garden is little more than 10 years old. Following tradition garden merges imperceptibly into farmed parkland with its planting of trees, singly and in groups. Very successful is a long formal vista on the west front. Balustrading, yew hedging, urns and obelisks give points of interest and four *Chamaecyparis lawsoniana* 'Kilmacurragh' provide Italianate exclamation marks. A huge carved head in a rondel (Lord Oxford from the now demolished Knightsbridge Barracks) is the final focal point reached through a wide double border of roses. He is backed by *Prunus cerasifera atropurpurea* (*pissardii*). Behind are plantings of shrub roses and peonies for a late June display.

Back by the house ground rises form a simple paved terrace on the south where *Helichrysum angustifolium* has seeded itself around and is clipped into hummocks; pinks and other grey-leaved things add to this scented area.

Further north are an enclosed swimming pool and a newly planted orchard; it is worth noting how the pears have been trained to weep downwards – lovely in flower and convenient for picking.

NOTEWORTHY SPECIMENS: *Quercus ilex.*

Upton Grey Place

Upton Grey, 4 miles SW of Alston and 6 miles SE of Basingstoke. Centre of triangle made by A339, A30 and A32.

When the owners moved from Upton Grey House 10 years ago to the new house they had built in their former kitchen garden across the lane, the move meant also an extraordinary change of ambiance. The old house was surrounded (and still is) by magnificent trees that were the product of 250 years of gardening and growth. The site of Upton Grey Place, by comparison, was almost treeless.

Hence the brief given to Messrs Russell who were chosen as garden designers was clear; quick clothing, a feeling of maturity, ease of maintenance and intensive summer interest based upon roses. The visitor a decade later can see how successful they have been. This is no esoteric plantsman's garden but one based upon broad concepts and well-tried plants.

Upton Grey Place is entered from its lowest point and the curving drive takes one up to the north (entrance) front of the house through broad banks of hypericum, *Cistus corbariensis*, lavender and potentilla.

Already roses can be seen to be a vital part of the plan. An 'Albertine' hedge, a depth of 'Penelope' and, around a seat, overshadowed by a healthy young *Magnolia grandiflora*, 'Lavender Lassie' and 'Chinatown'.

Walk round the potentilla banks between the house and the drive and the main garden becomes apparent. Here fine sloping lawns drop to the widest of shrub and rose borders. There are big groups of old-fashioned roses such as the Bourbon 'Fritz Nobis' and 'Souvenir de l'Imperatrice'. Further round is 'Buff Beauty' (whose fine foliage is ornamental long before the flowers appear) 'Marguerite Hilling' – the yellow 'Nevada'. Complementary herbaceous plants such as *Campanula lactiflora* are interplanted.

One mature tree has been used as a focal point; this is a remarkably regular mulberry and nearby are grouped rugosa roses such as the exquisitely scented 'Blanc Double de Coubert'.

Above and hence to the west of the house a border of gentle pinks and purples, softened further by grey foliage offers a summer treat. Here the roses progress from 'Rosemary Rose' through 'Perfection' to 'Plentiful'. Here too is bocconia, perowskia and cardoon for foliage effect with sedums and Japanese anemones for later interest.

The top of the garden appears to end at the old kitchen garden wall, but now beyond, in and amongst an old orchard, a new arboretum of interesting trees has been planted.

Vernon Hill House, Bishops Waltham

Leave Bishops Waltham on Cheriton road. Turn W. after 1 mile into Beeches Hill.

Vernon Hill is said to have been built by Admiral Vernon after the battle of Porto Bello which was fought in 1739, but periods both before and after that date have clearly affected the architectural scene. On the south, entrance, front, at the top of a steep gravelled drive the site and remains of a Victorian Gothic conservatory combine with the warm aspect to make a splendid group of tender plants survive and flourish.

Clearly they have not noticed the removal of the glass. Here is *Mandevilla suaveloens*, a huge Chilean jasmine; *Abutilon megapotamicum* with hanging red and orange bells; lemon verbena and oleander. A final pair are really surprising: *Cassia obtusa* (*corymbosa*) from Brazil and the perennial morning glory that is such a feature of Mediterranean gardens, *Ipomaea learii*. At Vernon Hill these two, the one golden yellow and the other blue-purple complement each other continuously from July to December. A nearby dry bank is wisely planted with cistus spp.

Behind the house plants and planting are more typical of Hampshire. On a north wall a high late Dutch honeysuckle overlooks a small rose garden with paved paths half-overgrown with thymes. The statuary here and elsewhere (including a pretty pair of moss-grown sphinxes) came from Lyme Park in Cheshire.

Lawns are on several levels backed by high trees — huge beeches, purple and green, cedars and other evergreens. A vista has been opened to the north enlivened by a recent pair of white borders. At their end a woodland area is entered and along the northern boundary a newly planted spring garden with camellias and later shrub roses. A remarkable feature is the thousands of naturalised early double tulips which, with the more conventional spring bulbs, make the season particularly worth waiting for.

The Vyne

Sherbourne St John, 4 miles N of Basingstoke. From A340 Basingstoke–Oxford road take National Trust signs to E.

This important early sixteenth-century house offers, in a short space, three distinct aspects of garden design. The visitor, approaching the main entrance front from the road sees an attractive typically Tudor brick manor house with associated outbuildings; great oaks frame the view across broad lawns.

But entrance is now on the west side. This low two storey wing is much more domestic in scale and to balance it the park is kept behind yew hedges inside of which is one of the best herbaceous borders in any National Trust property. Its potential in spring is exciting; its fulfilment in summer no less so and a labelled plan is available in the house for reference. Worth noting is the narrow paved walk between border and hedge for maintenance. By the door of this wing are a pair of old vines (*Vitis vinifera purpurea*) spirally trained up wooden wigwams, as a reference to the name of the house.

Reach the corner of the north front and the scale changes again, dramatically. Corner towers reach three storeys and in the centre the famous Corinthian portico (added incredibly early, in 1654). Here the eighteenth-century Landscape School takes over with broad sweeps of grass, carefully sited trees and views across the lake (a widened stream) to parkland beyond.

A walk to the left through mixed shrubs leads to a bridge crossing the lake; take the far path to see the house reflected and framed by fine trees.

NOTEWORTHY SPECIMENS: Phillyreas, stone seats in architectural yews.

West Green House

Signs to West Green turning N off the A30 1 mile W of Hartley Wintney.

As has been remarked before, it is surprising, for areas of the country so long settled, that neither Hampshire nor Dorset have the number of great country houses that certain others possess. Hence holdings of the National Trust are similarly small – The Vyne near Basingstoke is, of course, an exception of renown. From a garden point of view, West Green House, given to the Trust in 1957 by Sir Victor Sassoon, seems likely to be another.

The house itself, visually important from several parts of the garden, is of considerable interest. Of late seventeenth-century origin, with a deep wooden cornice and a hipped roof above its mellow red-brick walls, it is roughly square in plan. Few rooms are shown to the public, but visitors interested in house and garden relationships should not complain of this, especially as they look out from the exquisite saloon (an extraordinary grand room for a comparatively small house) which takes up the full two storeys of the west front and almost a quarter of the whole house.

While the house has, under its present tenants, been brought back to an eighteenth-century elegance the garden, originally not very exciting, is being developed under the same aegis in a number of interesting ways. Those areas against the house are acquiring architectural overtones, garden and park are being legitimately linked, the old walled kitchen garden is being replanted and a new pleasure ground (to use an eighteenth-century phrase) of a serpentine walk past exotic garden buildings around a small lake is in process of development. The whole concept is full of remarkable promise.

Entrance to the garden is across the gravelled north forecourt. To the right, through an iron screen, a new lime avenue is seen to end in a high eye-catching column. The visitor, however, is led up the north boundary along a dark hedged and walled alley watched over by the baleful gaze of a statue of Hecate at the top. (This three-headed monster originally came from Stowe). Here the orangery is entered and, dues paid (or National Trust card shown), the released visitor moves out into the world of light of a big upper lawn. Two grass terraces down is the famous west front of West Green House – windows on the ground floor but five roundels at first floor level containing busts of Bacchus and four flanking Roman emperors. Above the garden door a tablet is carved with the Hell Fire Club motto *Fay ce que vouldras*. Its presence here is unexplained and visitors are not encouraged to obey its maxim – at least on the premises.

At the top of the orangery walk a rustic garden-house holds the tombstone of a favourite spaniel of General Hawley, notorious owner of West Green House in the mid-eighteenth century. It reads:

> Oh Poor
> Monkey
> Come all yee shooters, come my losse bewaile
> The best black spaniell that ere wag'd a taile,
> Of questing Kinde and royall breed shee came,
> Great was her science, and as great her fame;
> Fifteen hard winters she did hunt, and last
> This stone's in memory of service past.
> Anno = 34
> I say no more

South of the garden-house the main west front vista crosses a ha-ha and is canalised across a meadow by a new avenue of sweet chestnuts. This, in 150 years time, should be worth coming a long way to see. From the openness of lawns and fields a wilderness garden is entered now at its north east corner. Here are good seasonal bulbs with, in May, quantities of fritillaries and in July, naturalised martagon lilies. At the time of writing this area is still in process of development. It has a central H-shaped pool, odd swells in the ground (probably spoil from the pond) and mixed shrubs and trees. The plan shows the intention to make the area more logically a part of the garden proper by cutting a path through the central bar of the 'H' and aligning this with a trompe l'oeil nymphaeum to the west and highest point of the garden.

The present path, of herringbone brick and inset millstones drops down from the pool to a moon-gate in the kitchen garden wall past clipped spheres of golden box.

At West Green House, kitchen garden is also flower garden, herb garden and fruit garden. In fact it could be regarded as a large and surreptiously sophisticated cottage garden. Basically a huge rhombus of sides about 80 and 60 yards in length; it is divided into six main beds with side borders against the walls of varying degrees of narrowness. This pattern was inherited as were three sides of fine brick wall and the fourth – the divide from the main west lawn – a screen of yews and other trees; this has been thickened in bosquets of hornbeam, Portugal laurel and further yew. Also inherited are the old apple trees around the paths which now not only fruit but provide support for roses and clematis. Each of the top two squares contain what can only be described as a fruit temple. 'Fruit cage' (for that is their role) is too prosaic a term for these elegant pleasure-domes of wood and wire. Thus viewed, red currants for instance, look just as ornamental as the enkianthus flowers to which they are often uncomplimentarily compared.

From these centres lavender-edged paths and rows of vegetables radiate outwards. Thus grown, even food plants take their place in the ornamental pattern. The cross walks of the lower four areas meet at a central feature. To the east the narrow near-enclosed herbaceous gardens are lightly planted with an emphasis upon pale-coloured flowers and interesting foliage.

On the west side a door leads to a natural tree-lined pool containing huge golden orfe and, most probably, waterfowl. It is for this particular interest that the tenants have taken in the south field to construct a lake with an island (approached by a Chinoiserie bridge).

Though still unfinished and not yet available to the public – such positively Stourheadian projects are not built in a day – the plan shows walks, trees, and amusing garden buildings of eighteenth-century elegance to enliven the way. Already duck and geese enjoy the water and cranes run in the long grass.

Returning back along the lower kitchen garden walk the west lawn garden seems almost austere by comparison and such contrast is an essential part of successful design. Through the arched brick screen are glimpses of the charming box parterre on the south front of the house.

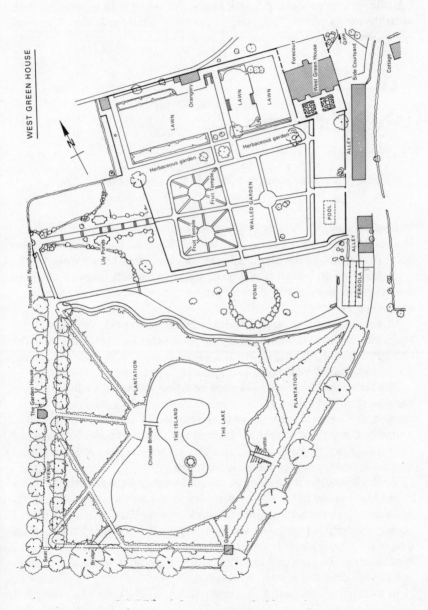

WEST GREEN HOUSE

Here too can be obtained the first full views of the west vista framed in trees and accentuated by statues. West Green House is a place where, happily, grand gardening is still being pursued yet in a personal and, with its use of plants, fully late twentieth-century manner. The complete concept is yet to be enjoyed.

Wyards Farm

1 mile W of Alton. From Alton take A339 Basingstoke road. First drive on left.

Past railed paddocks where elegant horses graze, the drive sweeps up by stables to the west front of the house. Wyards Farm is probably a place of pilgrimage for Janeites for it was here that Miss Austen wrote *Mansfield Park* in which her typical slightly waspish humour turns to deal its rapier thrusts at the social pretensions of the eighteenth-century landscape garden.

In the company of such shades it could be considered risky if not foolhardy to assay contemporary horticultural fashions; the novelist and her creations however are not likely to turn in their graves while success attends the efforts, and these are easy to see.

The stable buildings are enlivened by lawns and shrubs where a broad band of Jackman's blue rue is used to contrast with scarlet fosteriana tulips in spring. Beside the drive at the house is a screen of ceanothus – probably *C thyrsiflorus repens* – fronted with lavender and interplanted with *Lilium henryi*. Each of this trio gives a long season of interest and agreeable texture when flower is no more.

To the left of the front door at the main entrance side of the house a broad lawn gives views across a ha-ha to the chalk scarp beyond, its whiteness gleaming through the shallow soil. Here is a wide mixed border and opposite a generous planting of Rose 'Super Star' backed simply by a high beech hedge. (This screens the kitchen garden where, in addition to the conventional vegetables a speciality is made of flowers and foliage dried for winter decoration.)

In a corner of the lawn is a secret garden, a deep paved bay designed as a cool retreat for the hottest days. In the centre a tall old peach tree surrounded by cobbles now carries Rose 'Rambling Rector' while old-

fashioned rugosa roses crowd the back. Nearby a young davidia (handkerchief tree) does surprisingly well; it usually seems to resent chalk
soils.

The ha-ha is worthy of comment; so often a garden with the potential
of fine views is denied them by the need for a stock-proof barrier of some
sort. Jane Austen's landscapers knew the answer; sink the fence. But
then costs were seldom, it seems, such a problem – at least not in fiction.
Here, however, the perfect balance has been struck. The ha-ha is no
more than 25 yards in length while tree and shrub planting on both
sides curve in to conceal the stock fencing on each side and also
successfully to frame the view.

It is now best to return past the front door to the south front. Here
the area, enclosed by knapped flint walls, has been made over the last
five years into a most effective white garden. This is very much a
convention of our time but it is seldom so clearly realised, or put into
practice, that suitable foliage as a foil to white flowers is as important to
the final effect as the whiteness itself. Intended to be approached from a
glazed door in the house, the garden is centred on a rectangular pool
and its fountain, set in old York flags. Planting around is extravagant
with billowing hebes, hostas, rose 'Iceberg', lilies and so on. Soil is not
seen. *Romneya coulteri*, the lovely white Californian tree-poppy
succeeds so well as to become an embarrassment, but its heaps of
glaucous leaves are invaluable even when the flowers are over. Further
plants burst from the paving and clumps of *Yucca filamentosa* add
architectural point both in and out of bloom.

At each end of the pool are young trees of *Robinia pseudoacacia tort-
uosa* whose unusual shape and texture, particularly in winter, are
valuable. Beyond the south wall fields are half-glimpsed through a
screen of diffuse *Robinia* 'Frisia', and vertical chamaecyparis.Whiteness
on the house is continued with the best of the South American potato
vines, *Solanum jasminoides alba* (the commoner, hardier but coarser
S crispum is round the corner), myrtle and passion flower. If this climbs
into one of the robinias as is hoped the effect will be dramatic.

Wyck

3 miles E of Alton between the A31 and B3004. From Alton take the B3004 at turn N at East Worldham; Wyck 1½ miles.

With its dramatic setting amongst great trees, both indigenous and exotic, hanging on the flanks of a steep valley the equally dramatic east front of the house at Wyck makes a fine picture. Any formality of design that the garden possessed has mainly disappeared although the walled kitchen garden still has some good shrubs — eucryphias especially and fine hellebores in early spring.

It is at this time that Wyck may be visited for the drifts of naturalised bulbs on the valley sides. The display begins with a bank of aconites — perhaps 100 yards by 15 in extent under a grove of huge horse chestnuts (these in season must be magnificent). As the aconites pale, snowdrops take over, to be followed in mid-March by daffodils of the simple (and hence in such a situation the best) old-fashioned kinds. Crocuses and a few cyclamen add their distinctive brighter colours. Views to the south east are superb.

NOTEWORTHY SPECIMENS: *Liriodendron tulipifera*, *Pinus sylvestris* (*vast* Scots pine).

The Wylds

1½ miles north east of Liss. At Rake turn off the A3 W down Hatch Lane to T-junction. Turn right then fork left for Liss Forest and Greatham.

It is not often that one comes across what is virtually a new garden of some 40 acres. Not that the site of The Wylds is new. The Rev. Mr Cardew built a vast Victorian pile here — only a detached music room survives — and in the valley made a series of lakes. The biggest is about 10½ acres in extent (dug by hand, the local population were paid 4¼d per chain spit) and the others feed it. The succeeding 1930's house stands high on a peninsula above the water whose banks are planted with rhododendrons, beneath tall pines, and the effect is such that locally the area is known as Scotland.

The present owner, over the last ten years has cleared huge swathes of high *Rhododendron ponticum* and other scrub to transform the darkness of much of the planting with new extensive groups of modern deciduous and evergreen hybrids.

A serpentine drive a mile in length leads around the lakes to the entrance front of the house. From its garden front the ground slopes steeply to the water and in 1974 was planted with sweeps of ericas and callunas. Emphasis is as much upon coloured-leaved forms as upon flower and this extends the period of interest to almost 12 months.

A speciality of the new rhododendron planting has been with the modern small hybrids of *Rhododendron yakusimanum*. A temptation upon such obvious calcifuge soil (the ultimate in Bagshot Sands here) is to plant nothing *but* members of the ericaceae. At The Wylds mahonias (esp. *M.bealei x nepaulensis*) and *Viburnum tomentosum mariesii* are good and as ground cover *Cornus canadensis* and *Gaulteria procumbens* with bronze young foliage and fine red fruits should be noted in the stream garden below the house to the west. Also on the estate is a nursery which produces rhododendrons and camellias, mainly for trade sale.

NOTEWORTHY SPECIMENS: Fine mature beech (*not* just a chalk plant), oak, and conifers.

The Gardens of
the Isle of Wight

Cedar Lodge, Puckpool

From Ryde take Bembridge road and signs to Puckpool 2 miles. Cedar Lodge is on right opposite Puckpool Camp.

Mimosa seems almost to be the national flower of the Isle of Wight and nowhere is *Acacia decurrens dealbata* seen to better effect than at Cedar Lodge. The gravel drive which bisects the garden for its full length passing from the road to the stables is arched over first with holm oaks and then, inter alia, with mimosas; one has a trunk over a foot in diameter.

Ground slopes to the south east with many fine trees, notably a vast cedar which dominates the east lawn and gives the house its name. Emphasis has been put upon calcifuge plants which, given plenty of leaf mould, like the soil, and relatively tender things which are able to flourish here. Hence this is a plantsman's garden in which care has been taken to make the exotics and rarities look at home.

Left of the drive entrance a high copse gives light shade to some of the larger leaved rhododendrons and moving out into the sun is *R macabeanum*. As at Furzey (q.v.) the better plants of this great species seem to grow in the open: the Cedar Lodge specimen came from Appley Hall and may well be from Kingdon-Ward's original collections. Further down the slope south- and west-facing boundary walls are used for a range of tender plants: a particularly good trio are *Callistemon speciosum* (a scarlet bottle-brush) *Acacia armata* and the Trewithen form of *Ceanothus arboreus*. Nearby are both the wickedly spined colletias – *C.armata* and *C.cruciata*, the anchor plant.

Moving southwards the dominant plant is an enormous *Paulownia tomentosa* which covers itself with lavender foxglove flowers in May. Other trees in this area are young adult *Magnolia veitchii* and *M mollicomata*, at around 25 years beginning to flower well. Beyond is a clump of mimosa cleaned out to four main trunks growing out of the grass. These plants always look well; in flower in February and March they are a revelation.

The east boundary wall continues southwards and has fine climbers, notably *Bigonia capriolata*. Opposite, by the greenhouse, the particularly strong bamboo is *Arundinaria fastuosum*. It makes perfect protection and also provides dahlia stakes. The bottom shady corner has a collection of camellias and rhododendrons – the reputably tender *R fragrantissimum* types do very well here – and a walk leads up to the old stables and the drive again. Above, planting is dense on the west boundary with conifers, eucalyptus, *Viburnum rhytidophyllum* and *Parottia persica*.

A drainage ditch remains moist enough to permit a range of bog plants: both the lysichitums, astilbes, huge gunnera and, most unusually, the Chaltham Island forget-me-not, *Myosotidium hortensia*.

Returning back up the drive the wide border on the east has a number of good plants, but outstanding is a spreading group of *Melianthus major*, one of the best of foliage plants which here also flowers. Steps lead down to the house terrace, facing south across a long lawn. The drive border is supported by a stone retaining wall over which tumbles a range of herbaceous and shrubby plants. Ahead is an old open-ground *Magnolia grandiflora* and a towering willow. Only 30 years old, it now dwarfs the pond it was planted to complement.

NOTEWORTHY SPECIMENS: *Cedrus atlantica, Fagus sylvatica pendula, Paulownea tomentosa, Quercus suber* (Cork oak).

Dodpits House

Chessell Lane, Newbridge.W of Newbridge village off the B3401 4½ miles ESE of Yarmouth.

Here is a new garden on an old site of towards 9 acres with an emphasis upon interesting shrubs informally grouped in open meadowland – the once enclosing elms all now victims of the dread disease.

Ground slopes to the north east with open views to Shalfleet and Newtown. Visitors entering at the bottom should perhaps logically move straight up to the house (in the north west corner) via the grass terraces so that the garden is viewed first from where it was designed and from where it was planned to be enjoyed.

A little walled courtyard with a deep central well is the most protected spot and here the island's climate permits a fine *Cassia obtusa*, from North Argentina, a mass of gold from June to the frosts.

A door leads to the east terrace dominated by an enormous yew which has a developing hedge of golden *Elaeagnus pungens* in its shade. *Ceanothus arboreus* is on the house. It is from here that the new plantings are best begun. Fronting an old peach-lined wall to the left is a south-facing herbaceous border; ahead is a broad shrub border leading eastwards.

Emphasis is put upon certain genera: tree peonies, hebes, cistus, olearias. Subsequently, old-fashioned and shrub roses are planted in front of old orchard trees. A walk leads down along the eastern boundary with good plants all around. *Brachyglottis repanda* with its great felted leaves survives unprotected. At the bottom semi-natural pools are backed by an escallonia hedge and a collection of lilacs. Nearby are summer lilies.

From here walks lead back up towards the house through further young planting. Great care has been given to choice of species and also to their arrangement. Late in the year *Malus toringoides*, laden with scarlet fruit, is dramatically effective against the blackness of an old yew.

A particular interest is the wide collection, strewn about, of *Lavatera olbia*. This is a well-known and easy summer shrubby mallow; everyone else has been content with the ordinary type plant. At Dodpits variants collected all over Europe demonstrate the range of the species, thus worthwhile new cultivars of differing flower colour and so on will no doubt turn up.

NOTEWORTHY SPECIMENS: *Taxus baccata*.

Hamstead Grange

Nr Shalfleet, 3 miles NE of Yarmouth. Turn N at Shalfleet off A3054 Yarmouth–Newport road.

The great joy of Hamstead Grange is its position. After more than a mile of woodland drive the ground rises and through the gates the house is seen ahead. From its main terrace a superb view is afforded across farmland to the Newtown river, the Solent and, on clear days, the South Down ridge beyond Portsmouth. But to preserve this view means opening the garden on this side to the north-east and the terrace falls in three steps to a final swimming-pool garden in the protection of the boundary hedge. The house carries wisteria, lemon verbena and, in a sheltered corner, the tender *Jasminum polyanthum*.

On the south east front a formal rose garden is enclosed by a hedge of mixed *Cupressus macrocarpa, Thuya plicata* and Lawson's cypress. From here a walk leads back to a pair of natural pools near the gates, where in light woodland the ground is thickly carpeted in spring, first with narcissus and then with wild bluebells.

Shrubs opposite the entrance front of the house include good *Stransvaesia davidiana*, rhododendrons and *Acer palmatum*.

NOTEWORTHY SPECIMENS: *Pinus radiata*.

Lisle Combe

St Lawrence, 4 miles W of Ventnor, on main Undercliff road, A3055 midway between Ventnor and Niton.

The Undercliff on the Isle of Wight stretching westward from Ventnor to Niton offers a gentle microclimate almost unique in the British Isles. The high wooded cliff behind protects from north and east and so long as wind protection is obtained from the seaward side conditions are near-perfect. Frost is virtually unknown as is demonstrated by the garden front at Lisle Combe where Chilean jasmine (*Mandevilla suaveolens*) flowers and fruits, *Cassia obtusa* makes a big bush and under the open-fronted loggia ivy-leaved pelargoniums and *Tecomaria capensis* flourish without further protection.

Ahead, the ground drops away to a series of pools, and beyond a meadow the sea is seen. There are many plants of interest, often of enormous size. Just below the house a many stemmed *Cordyline australis* marks the head of the highest pool, water issuing from under the house. The pool, stocked with trout, has good growth of the South African water hawthorn, *Apotogeton distachyum*. To the right is a vast and highly productive fig tree.

Water descends to a second pool with a huge planting of *Gunnera manicata* to one side: pool edges are enlivened with candelabra primulas, arum lilies and other marginal plants. An east lawn has good groups of cistus and a number of interesting specimen plants: *Clerodendron fargesii* with flowers and blue fruits, *Griselinia littoralis*, a good sized Cork oak (*Quercus suber*) and *Phormium tenax* with long sword-like leaves and 8 ft high flower spikes. A shady dell under the cliff grows acers, camellias and spring bulbs.

The west end of the garden offers further things of interest with water-side plants and finally a small peat garden. Good trees include liquid-ambar, birches and parottia for autumn colour (though this is never dramatic in the soft climate), and a spreading *Cryptomeria japonica ele-gans* whose ferny growth does go a good bronze in winter.

Returning back up towards the house under a big cut-leaved beech an enormous clump of *Yucca gloriosa* is noteworthy especially when carrying a dozen or so flower spikes in late autumn.

The south-facing herbaceous border concentrates upon strong-leaved plants: *Melianthus major, Clematis heracleifolia,* peonies (tree peonies are a feature of Lisle Combe) and agapanthus combine well. West of the house is a formal rose garden and above is a rock garden where unlikely plants flourish. Here are aloes, *Agave america variegata* and the wickedly armed *Yucca whipplei* all rubbing shoulders with conventional ground cover.

NOTEWORTHY SPECIMENS: *Fagus sylvatica heteroplylla, Quercus suber, Platanus orientalis, Acer campestre.*

Little Brook

Brook, 9 miles SW of Newport on the B3399. 5 miles E of Freshwater and ½ mile inland from the sea.

This is one of several gardens in the grounds of a now divided big house, that of Little Brook itself surrounding a 1930's Regency-feeling house. The drive enters under a stand of huge Monterey pines and cypresses and it is interesting to note young bays and holm oaks with clumps of Acanthus flourishing in the heavy shade.

The main garden is to the south east and south west of the house, the former divided by a small but constant stream. This is bordered with ferns, bergenias, astilbes and montbretias. Kaffir lilies (*Schizostylis*) extend colour into December.

Beyond the stream yet hidden from the house is the kitchen garden backed by young Monterey cypress (*Cupressus macrocarpa*) – the mild Isle of Wight climate shows this plant at its best – and almost equally vertical *Pittosporum tenuifolium.*

On the south west front of the house a flagged terrace gives way to a croquet lawn flanked by shrubs and roses. These lead the eye to distant views of the sea. Against the house are further roses with *Nerine bowdenii* and enviably floriferous clumps of *Iris unguicularis* to carry interest through the winter.

Mottistone Manor

8 miles SW of Newport. On the B3399, 1 mile W of Brighstone.

Although the lovely stone house dates from the fifteenth and sixteenth centuries it declined in importance in later times and when it was restored by H.J.A. Seely (later 2nd Lord Mottistone) in the 1920's it had been a farmhouse for over 100 years. Hence the garden is of no antiquity: indeed it is only in the last few years that a garden worthy of the house has been developed. It is still very young.

The site is favoured: a narrow valley running northwards from the back of the house to thick woodland at the top. But its narrowness and steep sides combined with the fact that the house does not sit squarely at right angles has caused considerable difficulty in arranging the vistas. What has emerged is a series of three parallel gardens with the most important central one aligned from that window most continuously looked from – the kitchen.

These formal areas are approached by a broad flight of steps which act as a welcoming gesture from the entrance courtyard (itself entered through the arch of a great barn) and they lead to a grass terrace. On its left is a rose garden going up the valley on two levels; on its right, where the enclosing valley side is steeper, are several small terrace areas planted with fruit trees (including fine standard peaches) and underplanted in summer with vegetables. This brings the kitchen garden into the ornamental scene. And centrally, the main walk passes between a pair of long herbaceous borders. Enclosing hedges are of hornbeam and yew.

The walk moves into less formal surroundings as the valley narrows and leads away up to a semicircular stone seat (note the sea-horse supports) between an avenue comprised of differing pairs of fruit trees – quinces, plums, gages, apples and best of all for flower (though the birds get the fruit) sweet cherries; all are undercarpeted with spring bulbs.

This idea of using fruit as a part of the garden structure is a good and often productive one.

Turning about at the seat a fine view is obtained down the length of the garden, over the roofs of the manor to St Catherine's Down and the Channel. Moving right it is now possible to return down the valley on a 'shelf' halfway up its steep west side. Rough coppice has been recently cleared to give planting space for collections of rhododendrons, camellias, hebes and shrub roses. Behind, young conifers support the few old Scots pines that remain for wind protection. At the bottom are groups of evergreen azaleas; *Leptospermum scoparium* does well and indigenous bluebells cover the ground in May.

Back by the gravel court a good liquidambar grows by the stone barn and, on its southern side, a many stemmed *Myrtus apiculata* (*M.luma*) each, as always, a lovely cinnamon colour.

NOTEWORTHY SPECIMENS: *Pinus radiata.*

North Court

Shorwell, 5 miles SW of Newport on B3323 Newport–Brighstone road.

The fine Jacobean house stands proudly in its deeply wooded valley: everything is lush and extraordinarily green. The north, entrance, front, dated 1637, has an added Lutyens, though completely harmonious, wing of 1905. From here, across the drive, a broad meadow extends up the valley. Grazing sheep add to the timeless scene.

The garden begins on the east front, its porch dated 1615. Steps lead down to terraced lawns dominated by a vast larch and equally big specimens of *Platanus x acerifolia*. Half hidden is a domed stone pavilion which protects a clear spring into which steps descend for once convenient use. To the south, beyond a planting of cherries an equally crystal stream emerges from over-hanging branches and flows down the valley. It is backed by dense bamboos which provide staking material for the more formal parts of the garden. A stone bridge crosses the stream and leads to the village church. Further on, the stream can be re-crossed and then paths may be taken back to the south front of the house or up the side of the wooded hill that enclosed the valley on its west side. This serpentine path is lined with shrubs and trees and ends with a long grass terrace on the highest level, planted with flowering cherries in three forms. It overlooks the valley offering views across the village and, at its southern extremity, a glimpse of the sea.

From its north end a series of enclosed gardens are entered west and above the house which fall towards the high-walled kitchen garden. Here are herbaceous borders, venerable espalier apples and newly fruiting vines. The blue *Abutilon vitifolium* does well on the north side of the apple house; this is a particularly good form.

This perambulation misses the south front of the house. Here a box-edged rose garden is on the first level and on the next terrace level a formal pool set in paving.

NOTEWORTHY SPECIMENS: *Larix decidua, Platanus x acerifolia, Liriodendron tulipifera*.

Scotchells

Cheverton Shute, 1½ miles SW of Sandown on W side of A3056 Sandown–Newport road.

The drive to the thatched house is bordered by roses on one side and mixed shrubs backed unusually by a hedge of bay laurel on the other. An acid soil makes calcifuge things possible so that, not surprisingly, azaleas, heathers and camellias predominate.

North and east of the house the lawns are enclosed by conifers: when young, *Pinus radiata* is seen to be a remarkably ornamental plant, intensely green and clothed to the ground.

To the south ground falls away to a natural copse with a brook running through. This area is thickly planted with spring bulbs. Beyond are fine views to St Martin's Down, 970 feet high, with glimpses of the sea in the distance. Throughout the garden are bird boxes and feeders of many types and well over 50 species have been recorded here.

Steephill Botanic Garden

Ventnor. On A3055 Undercliff, Ventnor–Niton road, 1½ miles W of centre of Ventnor.

Municipal gardens do not easily come into the scope of this survey, catering as they usually do for a range of interests different from those provided for by the private garden. But Steephill is an exception in every sense of that word and the local luminaries of Ventnor should be congratulated now (as they surely will be in the future when things have grown) for making it possible.

When the 20 acres or so of grounds belonging to the defunct Royal National Hospital became available about 10 years ago the pressures on this unique site were considerable and various. It abuts the cliff-edge, yet is generally well protected, both from the sea and from the land sides; the long rectangle faces due south and is at the most southerly tip of the Isle of Wight. Should it become a building site, a holiday camp, an amusement park or merely a conventional public open space? Fortunately the botanic garden lobby won the day, the completely ruinous and overgrown acres were cleared of rubbish and the first new species (a now big *Drimys winteri*) was planted in October 1970. Development has been rapid, as has the growth of almost everything put in and already an extraordinary range of plants may be seen which compares favourably with the better-known climatically favoured areas of the Channel Islands and the Scillies.

From the car park against the road several paths descend into the garden but it is probably best to take the one near the centre which leads to the restaurant and bar (the stone plaques built into the front wall commemorate early benefactors of the hospital). From the terrace here forays can be made outward in three directions and also behind to obtain restorative sustenance when powers of horticultural credibility have been exercised beyond their normal limits.

Ahead, as an agreeable concession to non-botanical visitors, is a pleasant rose garden around a large oval pool. Planting is splendidly lush, with billowing lavenders as edges to the beds and enclosures of shrub- and old-fashioned roses. At its southern end, each side of a flight of steps a wide hedge of *R rugosa* forms and hybrids is spectacular both in flower and fruit. From the path thus reached, which extends the full length of the garden, ground rises again. This wide north slope is developing as a pinetum, though many of the most unusual and tender conifers are given woodland conditions elsewhere.

To the left of the rose garden a high wall and higher trees enclose an inherited palm garden of cordylines and trachycarpus. Other species of both groups have been added and to emphasise the tropical feeling, specimens of *Musa basjoo*, the Japanese banana, flower and fruit happily. Against the wall are young citrus – *C.ichangense* and *C.* 'Meyer's Lemon'. Behind are several of the South American climbing alstroemerias – *Bomarea spp*.

The palm garden adjoins an open lawn to the north of which a densely treed dell provides an area in which calcifuge plants succeed. Here a humus level has been built up above the limestone and clearly the opportunity was not to be neglected on this otherwise heavily limed soil. Shade is provided mainly by pines and *Cupressus macrocarpa*. (One monster was commemoratively planted on a visit to the hospital in 1897 by Princess Henry of Battenburg; it is fitting therefore that the Botanic Garden was formally opened in 1972 by her nephew The Earl of Mountbatten who is Governor of the Isle of Wight.) Here are some interesting young conifers: the Montezema pine and its close relative *P michoacana* whose leaves can be up to 15 in. long, for example, and the exquisite blue *Cupressus cachmeriana* looks like succeeding too. Odder are several Australasian podocarps and species of dacrydium.

South of the lawn a more open area possesses some of the plantings made in the botanic garden's earliest years. Mimosas are already 25 ft high. This area slopes upwards to the cliff edge and following it back westwards to the pinetum field fine views are obtained through the pines to the gardens and southwards across the sea. Below, a fault in the cliff has left a hollow shelf, perhaps 50 yards wide, which slopes gradually eastwards to the sea. This, too, will shortly be taken into cultivation.

However, keeping along the top of the main cliff a further area overhanging the main garden holds a range of interesting plants. At its end steps return to the main valley floor under mature pines now interplanted with the Balearic Island holly.

The visitor has now reached the western end of the main path first met by the rose garden and back along this path are some splendid plantings. To the left a high retaining wall with a broad border at its base holds, at present, some of the earliest and hence finest plantings of the new regime. *Cassia obtusa* (*C corymbosa* of gardens) romps away and is particularly effective in late summer with a purple vine scrambling through. *Albizia lophantha* has become 12 ft high and more than that thick. Even *Belaperone guttata*, the shrimp plant of our glasshouses and windowsills, has survived four years outside. A fine plant of *Myoporum laetum*, the 'Ngaio' of New Zealand, is interesting for its leaves studded with pellucid glands; naturally, this is only a plant for the mildest gardens. This border ends at the rose garden with a fine *Cornus capitata* which flowers and fruits well.

Turning left here and left again a parallel line is now retraced westwards above the retaining wall. This is a broad terrace of lawn, island beds and natural outcrops of limestone. On the latter an extensive rock garden has begun, generally of large-scale material which blends admirably into the scene; growth is predictably almost embarrassing, with *Ceanothus thyrsiflorus repens* having become 19 ft across in four years and other things in proportion.

Clearly, no written account can give any satisfactory impression of the wealth of fine plants to be seen here. Each visitor will find his own favourites, though this is at present rather fortuitous. Although the garden does not lack strong basic design the arrangement of material is somewhat at random. This is not to be surprised at; as a good site became available a good plant was immediately waiting to fill it (much material is from the Hillier Arboretum (q.v.) near Winchester). Hence unusual buddleias and other well-represented genera grow so far apart as to make comparison difficult. When, given time, order is superimposed upon the collections it can be foreseen that Steephill Botanic Garden will be famed not only in its own island but everywhere in the temperate world. Not least is its standard of maintenance; four men keep the garden impeccable – and this must be without herbicides for the range of plants makes any generalist treatment impossible.

Tyne Hall

Brembridge. In middle of village, at corner of High Street, turn down Love Lane. Entrance at far end.

The ninteteenth-century marine villa faces north with wide views across Spithead to the mainland. Hence, to keep the view open, ground to that side remains sheep-cropped meadow with large specimen trees.

On the south east front a central vista is contrived to pass through a formal rose garden, with its central pool, to a statue of Flora as 'Spring' backed by an apse of variegated *Euonymus japonicus*. Higher trees and shrubs on the boundary pile up beyond and massed bulbs at their foot complement the statue. Left of the rose garden an avenue of small flowering trees – malus and prunus – leads round to the east side of the meadow and drops down to a pillared garden house just above the sea. The walk is bordered by beds of mixed shrubs and roses: those things happy with marine exposure – hydrangeas, fuchsias, hebes and escallonias – predominate.

Returning to the east terrace a curved border to the right gives colour for a long season with herbaceous plants (*Agapanthus africanus* does well), roses and evergreen shrubs. Beyond, a good *Magnolia soulangeana* shows up against a high grey stone wall.

Hidden behind a golden yew hedge by the gravel entrance sweep is a swimming pool: the pavilion carries a mixture of *Solannum jasminoides album* and *S.crispum*. Other climbers on the house itself include *Hydrangea petiolaris* – taking full north exposure – and *Passiflora caerulea* which flowers well. Ripe fruits like golden bantam eggs hang on till Christmas. NOTEWORTHY SPECIMENS: *Cedrus altantica glauca* – youngish but freely coning, *Pinus radiata*.

Upper Chine School

In the old village of Shanklin on A3055 Ventnor road.

The school of some 350 girls is based primarily upon a rather grand stone house of 1874 with recent scholastic additions on the edge of the famed Shanklin Chine (a chine – the word seems to be restricted to the Isle of Wight and Bournemouth – is a deep wooded valley connected to the sea). The garden in outline is still that of a nineteenth-century private house with fine trees, rose walks and, at the entrance, areas of seasonal bedding.

From the house three bridges cross the chine, whose falling water can be heard at some distance. The main walk up the slope is bordered with pairs of trachycarpus palms and leads away from the garden to playing fields and the cliff-top. To right and left ornamental areas at a range of levels give views back to the house. In spring bulbs mass above the lawns to complement the cherries (there is good trio of our native

Prunus avium) and other early things.

Summer interest is provided by massed hydrangeas, and dahlias are grown in quantity as cut flowers for the house. The climate is mild enough for pelargoniums to be left out through the winter. NOTEWORTHY SPECIMENS: *Acacia decurrens dealbata* (mimosa). Courtyard and open ground specimens.

Westover

6 miles W of Newport. From B3401 Newport—Freshwater road turn S. Lodge is at bottom of Calbourne village.

This is a landscape garden of small size and great charm. The scene is set in the village of Calbourne with an octagonal flint lodge in front of a small lake. Hence the drive to Westover begins with a bridge crossing the outflow and it then climbs to the white Regency house on the rise.

On the south west lawn a broad ride leads down between old trees — oaks and very tall yews — and broadens out into an amphitheatrical dell. Perhaps it was a chalk pit. The sides are thickly planted as are a number of lower beds with a wide range of chalk-tolerant shrubs. Buddleias, philadelphus, deutzias and forsythias predominate.

To the left a path lined with young Japanese cherries ('Tai Haiku' and 'Shiro Fugen' amongst others) leads to what is apparently a garden temple. In fact it is a door made into the side of an old ice-house, presumably contemporary with the house itself. A steep path leads to the wood above the dell and others follow back to its floor through shrub roses and other plantings.

Retracing one's steps out of the dell a rising path to the left leads to a swimming-pool garden west of the house (the pavilion repeats the shallow pediment on the house itself). The pool is sheltered by the high wall of the kitchen garden to the north on which are trained magnolias. The kitchen garden, approached through a door in the wall, has trained fruits and dahlia borders.

NOTEWORTHY SPECIMENS: *Taxus baccata, Cedrus atlantica, Morus nigra.*

Index